D1648984

Seeing the Bible
Differently

How *A Course in Miracles* Views the Bible

by Allen Watson

#17 in a series based on *A Course in Miracles*

This is the seventeenth booklet in a series each of which deals with the modern spiritual teaching, *A Course in Miracles*. If you would like to receive future booklets directly from the publisher, or if you would like to receive the newsletter that accompanies this series, please write us at the address below.

The Circle of Atonement
Teaching and Healing Center
P.O. Box 4238
West Sedona, AZ 86340
(520) 282-0790, Fax (520) 282-0523
http://nen.sedona.net/circleofa/

ISBN 1-886602-06-10

Published by The Circle of Atonement: Teaching and Healing Center
Printed in the United States of America

Cover design and book design by Diane Goulder
Sedona, Arizona
(520) 204-2435

Table of Contents

-INTRODUCTION-

I have written this booklet from the perspective of many years of Bible study. Between 1957 and 1979, the Bible was my central source of spiritual teaching. From my late teens, I wanted to enter some kind of Christian ministry or missionary service, although I never did so. After college, I attended a full year of graduate work at a Bible college, where I studied New Testament Greek, Bible interpretation, and many specific books of the Bible. I read the Bible avidly: One year I read it through five times; usually I read it through at least once a year. For many years I led Bible study groups and taught the Bible in various churches. I owned more than a dozen translations of the Bible, and used them all in my study, often comparing versions side by side.

In other words, I was an extremely devoted, highly motivated Bible student. I expected to spend the rest of my life in its study. Furthermore, I believed it to be the final, only, and completely trustworthy Word of God, without errors. (That is one of the "fundamentals" of fundamentalists.)

Seventeen years ago I abandoned Bible study and began looking for spiritual truth in other places. Six years later I found *A Course in Miracles* and since that time, for eleven years, I have studied the Course just as assiduously as I used to study the Bible. I think this gives me a sufficient background to be able to speak with a reasonable degree of authority on how the Bible relates to the Course.

You may be wondering, "Why, after so many years of devoted Bible study, did you stop?" That is a reasonable question, and I think, before reading this booklet, it will be helpful to you to know a little more about where I am coming from. There are two sides to the answer.

First, despite many spiritual experiences during my years with the Bible, I was not happy. I had continuous ups and downs, with a preponderance of downs. There were some marvellous experiences of God's Love, but by and large the promises of the Bible, such as "peace that passes all understanding," or "life, and that more abundantly," escaped me. The Bible simply didn't seem to be delivering what it promised.

Second, and perhaps even more important, I was thoroughly disillusioned with every Christian group I had ever encountered. The best church contained only a handful who seemed to take the Christian message seriously. I saw hypocrisy, indifference, lack of any real communion with God, superficiality, and preoccupation with trivial issues of doctrine and practice everywhere I looked. I saw scores of divisions among followers of Jesus, most over the most petty issues—for example, whether or not it was permissible to fraternize with members of other Christian groups, whether you should baptize infants or only adults (and did you sprinkle or pour the water, or immerse people in it? If you immersed, did you do it face down, backwards, once, or three times for the Trinity, in standing or running water?). I saw, and also read of, families permanently torn apart by disagreements over such silly details.

I spent twenty-two years trying to get Christians to acknowledge their unity, and saw the most promising groups splinter and divide. There was even one group who ended up separating themselves from any Christians who did not overtly proclaim Christian unity! Seriously.

So, I had had it. I was at the end of my rope. I felt I was a failure, yet I felt that the church at large was even worse off. Although I retained an enormous respect for the Bible, it was clear to me that its teachings were not working, and rescue attempts seemed to be beyond all hope. I set it aside with great sorrow and regret, and began investigating what other teachings—spiritual and secular—had to say about God, truth and love.

When I first discovered the Course in 1985, God re-entered my life with a vengeance—or I should say, *without vengeance.* The Course seemed to me to embody everything I had always valued about what the Bible taught, without any of the elements that had dragged me down and divided Christendom. I devoured the Text when I began to read it, and have been studying it almost daily ever since.

I had some problems with the Course during the first few years. I had a lot of Christian baggage to dispose of. When I began to realize that the Course's teaching differed radically from the Bible in certain ways, I was not ready to give up the Bible doctrines. I had held them, unshakeably, for so long that they seemed like immutable truths to me. God didn't create the world? Jesus didn't bear my sins on the cross, suffering God's wrath in my place? Sin does not exist? My mind felt twisted out of shape. Most of all, I could not let go of my belief that the Bible was without error.

I kept reading the Course anyhow, ignoring the parts that I disagreed with. I kept reading because, despite my disagreements, something was happening to me. The joy and peace that had escaped me for my entire life until that point were starting to take hold and to become a more consistent part of my daily experience. My interaction with the Course was doing for me consistently what the Bible had done for me only for brief periods. In terms of the Bible story of the Exodus from Egypt to the Promised Land, I realized that I had finally left the wilderness, crossed the Jordan River, and had begun to possess the land of promise. At last—at long last!—I knew God and knew that I knew Him. I was home.

After about three years of reading the Course with reservations, one day as I was reading a passage that disagreed very pointedly with a central Bible doctrine (the reality of sin), I realized that not only did the logic of the Course on this point make sense to me, but I actually agreed with it. Sin *could not* be real if the separation never happened. I became aware that, without any struggle on my part, or without anyone's having attacked my biblical beliefs, my dedication to the conservative Christian theology on which I had based my life for so long was simply *gone*. The Holy Spirit had quietly, gently, changed my mind.

Despite what was a radical change in my beliefs, I never felt as though I had lost anything of value. I never felt a rupture between what I had learned from the Bible and what I found in the Course. For me, the Course seemed to complete the Bible, to explain it more fully, and to fulfill what it promised. My experience of the transition was that the Holy Spirit had simply purified my past learning and kept only the blessing, only what really worked. What was gone were the fears and the distortions. What remained was what the Bible, to me, had always been trying to tell me, but in pure, crystal clarity rather than muddy confusion.

My study of the Bible had led me to the Course. It had been the prelude to the Course; not something I now had to reject, but rather something I looked back on with gratitude for the way it had led me. Over and over again, I felt the Course confirming things I had seen (but only dimly) in the Bible. Then, I had seen "through a glass darkly," as Paul put it in I Corinthians. Now, the smudges and distortions were gone, and the message was as clear as day.

My personal history, obviously, is a powerful factor in determining the way I now see the relationship of the Bible to *A Course in Miracles*. I see the Bible as a preliminary, imperfect rendition of the truth, truth which has now been presented in a much clearer way in the Course. I retain a strong reverence for the Bible. I believe the truth is in it, but mixed with error. I believe that there can be great value in reading the Bible, for I believe the same Voice for God Who speaks in the Course *does* also speak in the Bible's pages.

Yet in the Bible, that Voice is muted with men's fears and mixed with men's imperfect perceptions. For nearly two thousand years the Bible was the clearest voice for God (at least in the West). Now, we have the Course— a more precise, more coherent presentation of truth. The Bible, therefore, is no longer necessary. It can, however, still be a valuable aid to our path. When Truth speaks in the Bible, it brings a message wholly consonant with the Course. Yet, in reading it, we need to discern between the Voice of Love and the voice of fear. We need to bring what we read in the Bible to the truth as given in the Course, rejecting the words of fear, and keeping only the clear message of God's love and forgiveness.

That is the general approach taken by this booklet. It is a middle road between two extreme positions I have heard among Course students. One group contends that the Course and the Bible are one hundred percent in agreement, and attempts to reconcile and integrate them into one another. Another group denounces the Bible as nothing but "the ego's religion," unworthy of any attention at all. I see the Course as a logical continuation of the Bible, growing out of it, agreeing with much of it, but gently correcting the Bible's mistakes and superseding it as a source of accurate spiritual teaching.

When I first wrote down the points I wanted to cover in this booklet, I realized I had written the outline for a full-length book, rather than a booklet. Some day, perhaps, I'll write that longer book. For now, however, I have chosen to compress and curtail what I want to say into this shorter form. As a result, some points are presented sketchily, with just enough support to make the point clear. Many examples, and many details of comparison between the Bible and the Course are not discussed at all. If I have omitted your favorite point, or your most burning question, I trust you will understand. I have tried to concentrate on the broader and more general issues, things that can serve all of us as guidelines in helping us, as students of ACIM, to relate to the Bible. I hope my readers will find this skeleton presentation useful and stimulating to their own thought and understanding

---

Note on Bible references: Quotations are given from both the King James Version (KJV) and the New American Standard Bible (NASB). The abbreviations are used to identify which version is being quoted.

-ONE-

The Importance of Their Relationship

Why is it important for students of *A Course in Miracles* to understand how the Course is related to the Bible? I see many reasons.

The Course Refers to the Bible Frequently

Dr. Kenneth Wapnick, in the Second Edition of his book, *Glossary-Index for "A Course in Miracles,"* lists (at a quick count) 881 passages in the Course that make direct or indirect reference to the Bible. That alone is enough reason for a careful student to want to understand how the two books are related.

When one book quotes or refers to another so frequently, the two books are obviously related in some way. The question is, how? Is the second book simply a continuation and expansion of the first? Or does the second book draw upon the first and build upon it, while significantly adding to and adjusting what the first book said? Or, perhaps, is the second book intended as a refutation of the first one?

The only way to determine the intended relationship is to examine, in the second book, how the first one is treated. Does it quote the first book approvingly, or critically? Does it merely repeat and elaborate on the earlier book, or does it offer corrections and additional concepts? That is how I have chosen to approach this subject: by looking at what the Course has to say about the Bible, and what attitude is taken by the Course towards the Bible and its teachings. Rather than simply offering my own opinions, I have tried to understand how the author of the Course views the Bible, and to communicate that as a guideline for us all. As students of the Course, the attitude taken by its author, it seems to me, should be the firm guideline for each of us in how we view the Bible.

The Course Freely Uses Biblical Terms and Symbols

The Course borrows many words and phrases from the Bible's vocabulary, such as, *Father* (in reference to God), *Holy Spirit, Christ, salvation, Atonement, forgiveness, altar, temple, Heaven, Son of God, crucifixion, devil, hell, sacrifice, sin, faith, Last Judgment, Second Coming, miracle, prayer, resurrection, angels,* and *revelation.*

To understand how the Course uses these terms, it is essential to understand the basic attitude the Course takes toward the Bible. If the books are basically identical, the meanings must be the same. If the books are in total disagreement, the meanings are probably opposite. If the two books are related in some progressive, complimentary way, then, very likely, the older meaning is the seed for a fuller, enlarged and purified meaning in the Course. Understanding the meaning of the terms in the Bible can enrich our understanding of how the Course uses them. In fact, simply comparing the usage of these words in the two books could tell us much about the fundamental relationship between the books.

The Two Books Share the Same Major Figure

The major figure in both the New Testament and the Course is Jesus. Both books claim to give the teachings of Jesus. The student, then, needs to determine for herself or himself what degree of authority to give to the two books. How do the books interpret the actions of Jesus and the events of his life? How do they present his teaching; do they agree, or do they disagree? And if they disagree, which one is the most accurate?

The Books Contain Many Similarities

In many ways, the two books agree in significant details. For instance, both treat the story of Jesus' crucifixion as an actual, historic event. Both teach that God is Love. There is clearly a kinship between them. We will devote a chapter to a discussion of some of these similarities.

The Books Contain Many Disagreements

On the other hand, on some points the two books just as obviously disagree. The Course speaks of "upside-down thinking in the New Testament" (T-6.I.15:1). It asserts that the disciples sometimes misquoted Jesus, and advises us as we read their teachings to "remember that I told them myself that there was much they would understand later, because they were not wholly ready to follow me at the time" (T-6.I.16:1). That statement is interesting for two reasons: first, because it seems to assume

2

that we *will* read the teachings of the apostles; and second, because it alerts us that the understanding of the apostles was not complete. We will devote another chapter to looking at some of the major disagreements between the Course and the Bible.

The Course Speaks to Those Within the Judeo-Christian Heritage

By and large the Course appears to assume that its readers are familiar with the Bible. It makes free use of its symbols and stories, sometimes with passing references, in a way that presumes the reader knows what is being talked about. For instance, Jesus speaks of a remark he supposedly made to Judas (T-6.I.15:4-9), and corrects some aspects of the biblical story. The paragraph would make little sense to a reader who had no knowledge of the events in the Gospels that are being referred to.

Interestingly enough, the Foundation for Inner Peace, who is responsible for translating the Course into foreign languages, has felt led not to translate the Course into languages whose cultures have no biblical background! Their contention is that it would amount to a double translation: first, attempting to translate the biblical concepts into ordinary language, and then attempting to translate the Course's use of them. In other words, their feeling is that without *some* background in the Bible, much of the Course would be nearly incomprehensible.

Many Course Students Have a Biblical Background

Those are the major reasons I see within the Course itself that seem to urge us to a clear understanding of the relationship between the Bible and the Course. Besides the reasons within the Course itself, there is the simple fact that so many of us who are now students of the Course came to it from a Christian, or Jewish, background. Our early religious thinking was formed of thoughts from the Bible. Is everything we learned there to be retained, or are there parts that need to be corrected? Or should we reject our biblical heritage entirely? Understanding how the Course is related to the Bible can help us answer these questions.

Some Course Students Desire to Remain Within Their Religious Heritage

It is very common for students of *A Course in Miracles* to wish to continue to participate in the activities of their synagogue or church. Often, there is great social value in doing so, or there are close family ties with people who still are practicing Christians or Jews. Furthermore, traditional religious groups offer meaningful ceremonies, give form to spiritual beliefs, offer concrete forms for the extension of love in the world, and give an opportunity for joining together in remembrance, service and celebration; things in which the Course community is noticeably lacking.

If the two books are completely irreconcilable, to remain part of these religious traditions seems inconsistent, impractical, perhaps hypocritical, and probably impossible for those who accept the Course as their primary path. If the two books are in total agreement, such continuing religious practice makes perfect sense. If the truth lies somewhere in between, then the question of membership in a church or synagogue becomes a problem to be settled on an individual basis, based largely on what is most expedient in each particular situation.

Relationships With Practicing Christians and Jews

Finally, settling for ourselves how the Bible and the Course relate can have an enormous impact on how we relate with practicing followers of the Bible. Do we see them as completely in error and needing correction? Do we see them as brothers and sisters on a path that differs only insignificantly in form from our own, but not in content? Or do we view them as people who share much in common with us, yet who also differ in significant ways—in forms and also in basic thought systems—but with whom we can join in recognition of similar content under the differing forms and thoughts?

My hope is that this booklet will give all of us a broad basis of understanding from which we can, each for ourselves, answer all of these questions.

Not Comparing the Course with Christian Theology

In addition, I want to make clear at the outset that this booklet does not attempt to contrast the Course and Christian theology; that has been attempted by several other books (mostly those by Kenneth Wapnick), and is surely worth careful consideration. We are, in this booklet, discussing how the Course relates to the Bible itself, not to theologies based on the Bible. There is, of course, some necessary overlap between these two topics, and theological differences will be touched upon, but the systems of thought based on the Bible (of which there are many) will not be our primary focus here.

-TWO-

How the Course Approaches the Bible

My general approach to our topic is to discover how the Course itself approaches the Bible. Let us, then, begin by examining an extended passage in the Text in which the Course specifically addresses, and reinterprets, four passages from the Bible. The passage is found in Chapter 5, Section VI, *Time and Eternity*, beginning with the fifth paragraph. From this section, I will attempt to derive some principles that can serve as guidelines for us, as students of the Course, in our reading and study of the Bible.

FOUR SAMPLE PASSAGES

The author has just pointed out, in the fourth paragraph of Section VI, how the ego uses Scripture for its purpose, and always interprets it fearfully. He then says:

> There are many examples of how the ego's interpretations are misleading, but a few will suffice to show how the Holy Spirit can reinterpret them in His Own Light (T-5.VI.5:1).

In other words, these passages are being examined for the very reason that interests us now: To show how the Bible has been misunderstood, and how the Holy Spirit can reinterpret it in a way that is more in line with truth. From these passages, we should be able to derive some principles about how the Course relates to the Bible in general, principles that we can then use to apply to the "many examples" of the ego's interpretations we may find in the Bible.

1. Sowing and Reaping

"As ye sow, so shall ye reap." This is not a direct quote from the Bible, but the idea is found in at least two places:

> They that plow iniquity, and sow wickedness, reap the same (Job 4:8, KJV).

> Be not deceived; God is not mocked: for whatsoever a man soweth, that shall he also reap (Gal. 6:7, KJV).

The fearful way the ego interprets this saying is fairly obvious: If you do bad things, you will be punished for it. More specifically, *God* will punish you for it. The common saying, "God will get you for that!" reflects this thinking.

The Course tells us that the Holy Spirit interprets these words quite differently:

> ...He reinterprets [these words] to mean what you consider worth cultivating you will cultivate in yourself. Your judgment of what is worthy makes it worthy for you (T-5.VI.6:1-2).

The general idea is still there, that what you sow (or plant) you will reap (or harvest). However, rather than a threat of divine retribution, the words become a simple statement of a neutral principle. The image of a vengeful God, just waiting to catch us misbehaving so that He can punish us, is entirely gone in the Holy Spirit's new interpretation. The "sowing" is something we do in our minds, rather than in our behavior; we "consider" something worthy, and we make a "judgment" about it. Ernest Holmes, the author of *The Science of Mind*, once stated the difference very clearly: "There is no sin but a mistake, and no punishment but an inevitable consequence" (*The Science of Mind*, p. 110f).

In the eyes of the Holy Spirit, the words, "as ye sow, so shall ye reap," become a statement of the oft-repeated law of perception in the Course:

> This is in accord with perception's fundamental law: You see what you believe is there, and you believe it there because you want it there. Perception has no other law than this (T-25.III.1:3-4).

Thus, if we judge attack to be what we want to see, we will see it; but if we want only love, we will see nothing else (T-12.VII.8:1).

For our purposes of trying to see how the Course approaches the Bible, what can we derive from this one example? First, we can see that the Course refuses to see anything that pictures God as vengeful. As we shall see, this is probably the single principle that most strongly governs the Course's interpretation of the Bible.

Second, we can see that the Course demonstrates, in this one example, four different types of relationship with the Bible. First, there is a *similarity* of meaning; the general theme of sowing and reaping stated in the Bible is carried over into the Course. Second, there is a clear *difference*; the Course's interpretation eliminates all trace of punishment from the idea. Third, there is a *continuity*; the Course is assuming the validity of the biblical statement, but is adjusting our understanding of it. Fourth, there is a *qualified supersession*; the Course presents its interpretation as higher, more correct, and one which is meant to take the place of the older understanding. We will see, in the remaining examples, that the Course consistently puts itself in relationship to the Bible in these same four ways.

2. Vengeance
"Vengeance is mine, sayeth the Lord" (T-5.VI.7:1).

Again, the Course is summarizing or abbreviating the biblical quote. The full quotation is:

Vengeance is mine, I will repay, saith the Lord (Rom. 12:19, KJV).

This line is, in its turn, a rewording of the original, given in the books of Moses in the Old Testament:

To me [belongeth] vengeance, and recompense (De. 32:35, KJV).

What is notable about the Course's version, first of all, is that it omits the words, "I will repay," which are attributed to God in the Bible. They carry the very clear idea that vengeance is not something for man's hands, but rather that God will repay, or adjudicate the recompense; in simpler words, God will take care of punishing evil, so leave it to Him. Once again we can see that the Course is deliberately removing any idea of a vengeful God.

The reinterpretation given by the Course makes use of one of its principle concepts: "that ideas increase only by being shared" (T-5.VI.7:1). The meaning of the primary thought, "Vengeance is mine," becomes, in this light, that "vengeance cannot be shared" (T-5.VI.7:2). We should, therefore, "Give it…to the Holy Spirit, Who will undo it in you because it does not belong in your mind, which is part of God" (T-5.VI.7:3). Instead of giving vengeance into God's hands so that He can carry it out, we give it to the Holy Spirit to be *undone*! In fact, the reason that vengeance does not belong in our minds is that our minds are part of God—which obviously implies that vengeance has no place in God's Mind, either.

Notice that this can hardly be said to be the meaning that was in the mind of the Apostle Paul when he wrote the Epistle to the Romans. Although he is clearly teaching Christians not to avenge themselves (see Rom. 12:18), he continues after the verse quoted above:

> If thine enemy hunger, feed him; if he thirst, give him to drink: for in
> so doing thou shalt heap coals of fire upon his head (Rom. 12:20, KJV).

His thought seems to be that if you return good for evil, you will be in effect calling down God's wrath on the person who offended you, symbolized by coals of fire pouring onto his head!

In this passage we once again see the four ways the Course relates to the Bible. *Similarity*: do not avenge yourself, but give vengeance to God. *Difference*: we give the vengeance to God, not to be carried out more effectively by Him, but to have it removed from our minds entirely. *Continuity*: the Course does not reject the teaching, but gives it a new meaning. *Qualified supersession:* the Course presents its teaching in place of that of the Bible, but still somehow in line with it.

3. Inherited Sin

The Bible seems to teach that sin is so terrible that punishment for it falls not only on the person who did it, but lives on as a kind of curse upon succeeding generations: "I will visit the sins of the fathers unto the third and fourth generation" (T-5.VI.8:1). Again, this is an abbreviation of the original quote, which can be found in Exodus 20:5 and 34:7. The Course sees this understanding as "merely an attempt to guarantee the ego's own survival" (T-5.VI.8:2). This is in line with the Course's teaching elsewhere (T-13.IV.4:4-5) that the whole idea of paying for the past in the future is the ego's way of avoiding the present, which is the only time in which healing can occur.

The ego's interpretation of these words "is particularly vicious" (T-5.VI.8:1), says the Course. Such a teaching portrays a mad god, one who punishes children for their father's mistakes, which seems manifestly unfair and spiteful even to our less-than-divine minds. The Course simply cannot tolerate such an image of God. It gives the Holy Spirit's radically different understanding:

> To the Holy Spirit, the statement means that in later generations
> He can still reinterpret what former generations had
> misunderstood, and thus release the thoughts from the ability to

produce fear (T-5.VI.8:3).

Instead of meaning that punishment is carried out down through the generations—a horrible concept!—it now means that in later generations, God's mercy can still reach out and heal the thoughts of those former, mistaken, generations. The present generation, rather than having the sins of their fathers visited on them, is released in the present from the fear those "sins" have produced.

Once again, let me point out that the authors who penned the Old Testament did not in any way share this merciful understanding! No one familiar with the early books of the Bible, with their descriptions of the plagues and curses that would fall on those who disobey God, could have the slightest doubt that those authors really believed that God would punish sin down through the generations. (If you want a gruesome example, read Deuteronomy 28:15-68; fifty-four verses detailing the curses God will visit on unbelievers, including pestilence, draught, death in battle with your carcass becoming food for the birds, boils, hemorrhoids, madness, blindness, having your wife raped, and slavery.) After a long list of curses, the Bible adds, "And they shall become a sign and a wonder on you and your descendants forever" (De. 28:46, NASB), making it clear just what the Old Testament authors believed about God visiting the sins of the fathers upon their children.

When the Holy Spirit says, "Its real meaning is this," He cannot be referring to what was actually in the thoughts of those who penned the words. He must be referring to what the original thought was, in God's Mind, which was distorted almost beyond recognition by those who heard it before it was recorded in the Bible. This concept, that the "true meaning" is not necessarily what was in the authors' minds, but refers to God's original revelation, is a key to understanding how the Course treats the Bible.

It also clearly demonstrates the principle of *qualified supersession* I have referred to with the earlier passages; the Course claims the authority to tell us what God's original intent was behind the garbled understanding of the biblical authors. It acknowledges that, behind those words, revelation was at work. Yet it perceives that the revelation was distorted, and that the Bible's rendition of it needs to be purged of its fearful elements and restated more clearly for our benefit.

The other three ways the Course relates to the Bible are also present in this passage: *similarity*, in the idea of something being carried down the generations; *difference*, in that what is carried is not vengeance carried forward, but mercy carried backward in time; and *continuity*, in that it is the same revelation being discussed, but given an entirely new meaning.

4. The Wicked Perishing

The last Bible statement treated in this section is, "The wicked shall perish" (Ps. 37:20, KJV). The old meaning should be obvious, referring to wicked souls receiving death and punishment in hell. The Course interprets it to mean, "Every loveless [or, wicked] thought must be undone" (T-5.VI.9:2). The transfer of meaning from persons, or souls, to *thoughts*, is something that may be a familiar interpretation device to those who have approached the Bible from a New Thought background (Religious Science and The Unity School of Christianity, for instance). The Course uses it again in reinterpreting the meaning of the Last Judgment, in Chapter 2, Section VIII of the Text, where it is portrayed as a final evaluation of our *thoughts* in which we retain only what is creative and good, rather than a time when good and bad *souls* are separated into Heaven and hell. The Bible's constant pronouncements of judgment on evildoers can actually become meaningful discourse about correcting our thinking through use of this interpretive device, just as the Course does here.

The same elements of interpretation are present in this fourth example: *similarity*, in that something "wicked" must be brought to an end; *difference*, in that what are ended are loveless thoughts rather than loveless people; *continuity*, in that the older expression of truth is not nullified but uplifted; and *qualified supersession*, in that the Course's interpretation is given in place of the old, yet is based upon the same general idea.

Overall, as in the earlier examples, the central idea that the Course attempts to eradicate from our understanding seems to be the idea of a God of wrath, Who punishes us for our evil deeds. That theme is so central to understanding how the Course views the Bible that it deserves a more thorough discussion.

"JUDGMENT IS NOT AN ATTRIBUTE OF GOD."

The Text tells us flatly that, "Judgment is not an attribute of God" (T-2.VIII.2:4). It speaks of "...your delusion of an angry god, whose fearful image you believe you see at work in all the evils of the world" (W-pI.153.7:3). It tells us that illness results from the ego's attempt to punish itself in order to avert God's punishment:

> The ego believes that by punishing itself it will mitigate the punishment of God. Yet even in this it is arrogant. It attributes to God a punishing intent, and then takes this intent as its own prerogative (T-5.V.5:6-8).

Nestled in there is the clear statement that the very idea of a punishing God is something attributed to God by the ego, and not something that has any basis in truth. To the Course, the idea that punishment is a form of correction is insane (T-19.II.1:6). It is one of the laws of chaos (T-23.II.4) upon which the entire ego thought system is built.

In discussing the idea that justice and vengeance are not synonymous, the Course tells us: "Vengeance is alien to God's Mind *because* He knows of justice" (T-25.VIII.5:5). To our ego minds, justice means that we are punished for our sins. To the Course, justice means *not* punishing us because we have *not* sinned.

The Bible's theology is based upon a two-faced concept of God, in which He is both loving and vengeful at the same time. In the Bible's eyes, although God loves us all, somehow He is forced, by His concept of justice, to punish us for our sins. The Course sees God with a single eye: He is Love, and Love without any opposite. That foundational idea seems to govern every instance in which the Course reinterprets the Bible, as we shall see in the remainder of this booklet.

Conclusions

We have seen how the Course relates to the Bible in four different ways. There are similarities, differences, continuity, and qualified supersession. We can even see these four relationships in the concept of God we have just discussed. The similarity is that both the Bible and the Course present God as a loving God; the difference is that the Bible *also* presents God as wrathful and punitive; the continuity is that *A Course in Miracles* sees itself as standing in the same line of revelation about this God; and the qualified supersession lies in the way the Course sees its teaching about this God as more authoritative than the Bible's. The next four chapters will deal with each of these relationships in expanded form. And through them all, we will see the concept of a God of pure Love, to Whose Mind vengeance is an alien thought, applied again and again to the ways we have misunderstood His message to us.

-THREE-
Similarities Between the Course and the Bible

GOD IS LOVE

In the Bible, I John 4:8 and 4:16 declare, "God is Love." With this teaching the Course is in complete agreement; it directly quotes the line at least seven times, for instance:

> God is Love and you do want Him (T-9.I.9:7).

> And there are overtones of seeming fear around the happy message, "God is Love" (T-29.I.8:7).

> He will appear when you have answered Him, and you will know in Him that God is Love (T-31.I.10:6).

> God, being Love, is also happiness (W-pI.103; several repetitions).

The thought, "God is but Love, and therefore so am I," is given as a daily thought for ten lessons in Review V of the Workbook.

The Course does not deviate from this idea; here it is in total agreement with the biblical teaching. What the Course bases on this idea—for instance, the thought that since God is Love, we too, as His creations, must also be Love—often consists of ideas not found in the Bible, or even contrary to it. When the Course says, "God is but Love," it means, "God is *only* Love." The Course rejects everything that might be inconsistent with this view of God; for instance, the idea that God might want to punish us for our "evil deeds," or even that He might want to punish Jesus in our place. The whole idea of vengeance, or even of sacrifice, is incompatible with the Course's picture of God as Love.

The picture of God, often found in the Bible, as loving, merciful, and wholly benevolent, is totally confirmed by the Course. Even in my

13

Christian days, when my thoughts about God were based completely on what I saw in the Bible, I came to believe that nothing could possibly separate us from God's Love:

> For I am convinced that neither death, nor life, nor angels, nor principalities, nor things present, nor things to come, nor powers, nor height, nor depth, nor any other created thing, shall be able to separate us from the love of God... (Rom. 8:38-39, NASB).

THEIR VIEW OF HISTORY

By "view of history," I mean the way that the Bible and the Course view the totality of human history. Some religions, such as Hinduism, view history as cyclical, with something like a pendulum swing from unity and peace in the divine One, to separation and discord in "maya," or the illusory world, and back again. In contrast to this, both the Bible and the Course share an overall picture of human history that seems to have a distinct beginning and a distinct ending, with the ending being final, the story not to be repeated endlessly.

The biblical account tells us that there was, in the beginning, an original harmony, followed by a "Fall" from grace in the Garden of Eden. Since then, under the guidance of a divine plan for salvation, there has been a gradual returning to God, beginning with a few individuals, then the offspring of Abraham, which became the tribe of Israel, and finally a powerful nation under King David and King Solomon. The nation failed God, divided, went into captivity, and were still serving under foreign rulers when Jesus appeared. His appearance was pivotal to salvation's plan. Through the preaching of his message, and through his Apostles, the Kingdom of God was extended beyond Israel to the "Gentiles" (non-Israelites), and—according to the visions of the New Testament teachers—will eventually encompass all of (redeemed) mankind. The history of the world will culminate in a great conflict between forces of good and evil, in which good will triumph. Then, according to some interpreters, after a 1000-year reign of Jesus and a Last Judgment in which the sinful will be banished to hell, the world will finally end in the creation of a new Heaven and new Earth, with the two joined in one under God's authority.

Whatever their choice of details, most biblical scholars agree that history moves from the blissful beginning, into the Fall, through a process of salvation, to a final, glorious ending in the Kingdom of God.

Although the Course's understanding of the details differs greatly (see "The Fall" in the next chapter, for instance), its basic picture is the same: original creation was a perfect harmony and unity. Human history began with what the Course calls "the separation," which was immediately answered by God's plan for salvation. History moves through an Atonement process, hinging on the appearance of Jesus (just as in the Bible), and finally culminates in the "real world," the union of all things in Christ (the Second Coming), a Last Judgment (one that bestows a gift of correction rather than a verdict of condemnation), after which the world simply disappears, and the original harmony is restored, or recognized as having never been disrupted in truth. The close similarity of this scenario to that presented in the Bible is somewhat comforting in its familiarity for those coming from a background of Bible teaching, and is actually quite unique among world religions. (Islam, which also shares a biblical heritage, of course shares this general view of history.)

The major difference between the historical views of the Bible and the Course lies, not in the overall scenario, but in their views of the God who directs the process of salvation (Love, not judgment), and the reality (or lack of it) accorded to the Fall, or separation, which is being corrected throughout history. To the Bible, mankind's fall and return are very real; to the Course, they are only an imaginary journey in a nightmare.

FORGIVENESS

As any student of the Course quickly realizes, forgiveness is its central teaching: "Forgiveness is the central theme that runs throughout salvation" (W-pI.169.12:1). The Bible also makes forgiveness a central issue, although it differs in the basis upon which forgiveness is attained (see next chapter). The first Christian sermon, delivered on the day of Pentecost, ended with the admonition to "be baptized in the name of Jesus Christ for the forgiveness of your sins" (Acts 2:38, NASB). Jesus, in the Gospels, frequently told those who came to him, "Your sins have been forgiven." The book of Hebrews in the New Testament declares that with real forgiveness, it is possible to live with "no consciousness of sins" (Heb. 10:2, NASB) and without need of any further offerings (sacrifices or payments) for sin (Heb. 10:18, NASB).

In the Old Testament, God is quoted as telling His people that their sins have been removed from them "as far as the East is from the West" (an infinite distance, Ps. 103:12, NASB), or cast into the depths of the sea

(Mic. 7:19), so that God will "remember their sin no more" (Jer. 31:34, KJV). The Apostle Paul declares, "There is therefore now no condemnation for those who are in Christ Jesus" (Rom. 8:1, NASB).

In my own experience, one of the great truths I began to learn in my Christian days was that God did not want to punish me for my sins, but that He had made a way in which they could be wiped from the record, totally expunged, gone and forgotten forever. I came to believe that God saw us—all of us—as sinless. While I am quite clear, as I have already said, that the basis upon which forgiveness is grounded in the Bible is very different from the basis given it in the Course (discussed in the next chapter), nonetheless, the promise of complete freedom from guilt is identical in the two books.

THE IMPORTANCE OF JESUS

Clearly, one of the greatest points of similarity between the Bible and the Course is the importance they both give to Jesus as the central figure in the unfolding drama of redemption. His appearance in the world, his life, his death, and his resurrection were in some way, for both books, the linchpin of history, the key to God's plan to bring mankind back to Himself.

The Bible calls Jesus the "captain" of our salvation (Heb. 2:10, KJV); in the Course, he says, "I am in charge of the process of Atonement, which I undertook to begin" (T-1.III.1:1). In some way, Jesus brought the Holy Spirit into the world in a new way: the Bible says he sent the Holy Spirit to us from Heaven (John 16:7, NASB); the Course says he "called down [the Holy Spirit] upon the earth after he ascended into Heaven" (C-6.1:1).

The Course says that Jesus' resurrection established the Atonement (T-3.I.1:2). When Jesus rose from the dead—a fact both books agree on—something profound happened for all of us. The Bible says we are "risen with him" (Col. 2:12, KJV), and that in some way, when he rose, we also rose, and are seated with Christ in heaven (Eph. 2:5-6). In the Course Jesus says:

> I will awaken you as surely as I awakened myself, for I awoke
> for you. In my resurrection is your release (T-12.II.7:2-3).

Thus, both books attribute profound importance to Jesus and his historical life.

In addition, both books ask us to view Jesus with a great deal of respect and even reverence. The Bible refers to him as "Lord" and asks us to obey him. Even in the Course (T-1.II.3:6-8), Jesus asserts that, due to his greater experience and greater wisdom, he is entitled to our respect, our obedience, our love, and our devotion. The Course, in fact, even asserts, much as the Bible does, that we can use his name in prayer in place of any of the names of God we have learned:

> The Name of Jesus Christ as such is but a symbol. But it
> stands for love that is not of this world. It is a symbol that is
> safely used as a replacement for the many names of all the gods
> to which you pray (M-23.4:1-3).

Thus, while asserting our equality with Jesus in eternal reality, and our eventual equality at the end of time, the Course does accord Jesus a very high place as a symbol of God Himself, one to whom prayers can be directed, and tells us he is "in charge of the Atonement" (T-4.VI.6:5).

There are even some passages in the New Testament that seem to hint, fairly clearly, at a teaching similar to that of the Course: that all of us are equal to Jesus. For instance:

> Beloved, now we are children of God, and it has not appeared as
> yet that we shall be. We know that, if He should appear, we shall
> be like Him, because we shall see Him just as He is (I John 3:32,
> NASB).

Peter says that we have "become partakers of the divine nature" (II Peter 1:4, NASB). And in the Gospels, Jesus himself admonished a man who called him "Good Teacher," pointing away from himself to God: "Why do you call me good? No one is good except God alone" (Mark 10:18, NASB). These teachings seem inconsistent with the emphasis elsewhere on Jesus' uniqueness, and the frequent references (especially in Matthew) to those who "worshipped" him, yet to be fair, we must admit their counteracting presence in the Bible. To me, it seems to indicate that there may have been a deeper understanding of some things, early on, that got diluted down through the years before the Bible was produced in its present form.

THE IMPORTANCE OF THE HOLY SPIRIT

In the Bible, the term "Holy Spirit" seldom occurs at all. Surprisingly, the term occurs only seven times in the King James Version of the Bible; three times in the Old Testament and four in the New. The term "Spirit of God," however, occurs much more frequently: fourteen times in the Old

Testament, and twelve times in the New. The King James Bible, however, uses the phrase, "Holy Ghost" (which is synonymous with "Holy Spirit") eighty-seven times, mostly in the New Testament. Thus, the Holy Spirit is much more a phenomenon of the Christian era.

This makes sense, because the Christian era was inaugurated, according to the "Acts of the Apostles," by a significant new "outpouring" of the Holy Spirit on the disciples of Jesus on the day of Pentecost. In the Bible, Jesus promises this special advent of the Holy Spirit to his disciples:

> And I will ask the Father, and He will give you another Helper,
> that He may be with you for ever; that is the Spirit of truth,
> whom the world cannot receive, because it does not behold Him
> or know Him, but you know Him because He abides with you,
> and will be in you (John 14:16-17, NASB).

Jesus is telling his followers that the Spirit Who was now *with* the disciples would soon be, not only *with* them but *in* them, in some new way. Jesus even states that the presence of the Holy Spirit will be of more value to the disciples than his own continued presence would be: "I tell you the truth, it is to your advantage that I go away; for if I do not go away, the Helper shall not come to you; but if I go, I will send Him to you" (John 16:7, NASB). In the book of Acts, which tells the story of the early years of the church, phrases like "led by the Spirit of God" or "filled with the Holy Ghost" occur dozens of times; the whole expansion of the church is presented as an activity of the Holy Spirit through the disciples.

A Course in Miracles seems to share this same sense of the importance of the Holy Spirit to those who follow its path, and even to give Him greater importance. The term occurs in 758 places in the Course material (counting the two supplemental pamphlets). Without the Holy Spirit, there would simply be no escape from our illusions of separation:

> The Holy Spirit is God's Answer to the separation; the means by
> which the Atonement heals until the whole mind returns to
> creating (T-5.II.2:5).

> ...God's Will cannot be forced upon you, being an experience of
> total willingness. The Holy Spirit understands how to teach this,
> but you do not. That is why you need Him, and why God gave
> Him to you. Only His teaching will release your will to God's,
> uniting it with His power and glory and establishing them as
> yours (T-8.III.2:3-6).

Yet can you find yourself in such a world? Without the Holy
Spirit the answer would be no. Yet because of Him the answer is
a joyous yes! (T-13.VII.10:6-8)

You have set up this strange situation so that it is impossible to
escape from it without a Guide Who does know what your
reality is (T-9.I.3:5).

Both the Bible and the Course refer to the Holy Spirit by the pronoun,
"He," attributing personhood[1] to Him. Both describe Him as a Guide, a
Comforter, and the One who can direct us in every area of our lives. In
both, the Holy Spirit seems to be the activating power of God, working
within this world, to teach us and lead us home to God. In both books, the
Holy Spirit is said to be *in* us in a literal sense, somehow a part of us, yet
also a part of God, acting as a communicating link between the Father and
His separated children.

ONENESS AND THE GOAL OF UNION

Another major teaching in which I feel that the Course and the Bible
clearly echo one another (though not everyone would agree with me) is that
of the underlying oneness of all things in God, and the goal of returning all
of creation to an awareness of that oneness. The teaching of oneness began
in the Old Testament when Moses declared, "Here, O Israel! The Lord is
our God, the Lord is one!" (Deut. 6:4, NASB). I learned, in my days of Bible
study, that the word "Lord" stood for "Jehovah," a singular noun, while the
word "God" here stood for "Elohim," a plural noun. This statement was not
simply saying, "There is only one God." It was saying that God is a
compound unity, a Whole consisting of many parts.

In his sermon to the pagans in Athens, a city full of many idols, Paul the
Apostle referred to an idol that was inscribed, "To an unknown God." He
told the Athenians that God "gives to all life and breath and all things," that
he made every nation of mankind from one (or one blood), and then
declared, "He is not far from each one of us; for in Him we live and move
and exist" (Acts 17:16-28, NASB). That final statement is echoed in the
Course in many different places:

God is All in all in a very literal sense. All being is in Him Who
is all Being. You are therefore in Him since your being is His
(T-7.IV.7:4-6).

...the Voice that speaks for God in everything that lives and shares His Being (T-24.VI.5:6).

Clear in Your likeness does the Light shine forth from everything that lives and moves in You (T-31.VII.12:7).

You cannot walk the world apart from God, because you could not be without Him. He is what your life is. Where you are He is. There is one life. That life you share with Him. Nothing can be apart from Him and live (W-pI.156.2:4-9).

We live and move in You alone. We are not separate from Your eternal life (W-pI.163.9:3-4).

God is with me. I live and move in Him (W-pII.222.Title).

The Bible teaches that all things "consist" (KJV) or "hold together" (NASB) in Christ (Col. 1:17), and that Christ "is all, and in all" (Col. 3:11, NASB). In simple terms this seems to be saying that Christ is all there is (at least that he is all of creation), something the Course would agree with. "You are a child of God, a priceless part of His Kingdom, which He created as part of Him. Nothing else exists and only this is real" (T-6.IV.6:1-2).

Besides sharing this vision of the unity of all things in God, both the Bible and the Course see the process of salvation or redemption being one in which the apparently separate parts of creation are moving inexorably back to an awareness of oneness and unity. The goal of salvation in I Cor. 15:28 is "that God may be all in all" (NASB).

In the long prayer of Jesus, just prior to his crucifixion, we read these words in John's Gospel:

> "I do not ask for these alone [his contemporary disciples], but for those also who believe in Me through their word; that they all may be one; even as Thou, Father, art in Me, and I in Thee, that they also may be in Us...that they may be one, just as We are one; I in them, and Thou in Me, that they may be perfected in unity..." (John 17:22-23, NASB).

The Bible tells us that God is breaking down all barriers of separation, between man and God and also between men and other men (and between men and women, for that matter); He is making them "into one new man" (Eph. 2:15, NASB). Paul compares the church to the "body" of Christ (Eph. 1:22-23, NASB) in which we are all "members one of another" (Rom. 12:5, NASB), mutually interdependent. He says we are "being built together into a dwelling of God in the Spirit" (Eph. 2:22, NASB). The Bible contains a vision—although rarely seen or taught by Christian churches in my experience—of a corporate salvation, an ending of all separation. That vision is clearly shared by the Course, although with an even more inclusive perspective. In the Book of Revelation, the New Testament ends with a vision of the New Jerusalem, in which all believers are united at last in glorious unity under the headship of God. Yet the same book tells of those left outside the holy city, consigned to "the lake that burns with fire and brimstone" (Rev. 21:8, NASB). The Course allows for no exclusion; everyone will at the last be joined in God. "...the lack of exceptions is the lesson" (T-7.XI.4:2).

---

[1] Personhood, certainly, but not masculinity. For a discussion of the Course's use of masculine pronouns in reference to God and the Holy Spirit, see Robert Perry's *A Course Glossary,* under the entry for "He-Him." This book is available from The Circle of Atonement.

-FOUR-
Differences Between the Course and the Bible

Despite the fact that there are quite a few profound agreements between the Course and the Bible, as we have seen in the last chapter, it is far easier to find differences between the two than to identify the similarities. This is due, in no small part, to the fact that the Course goes to some lengths to point out the differences!

The differences are numerous, and we cannot possibly enumerate them all in this short chapter, so we will content ourselves with pointing out some of the most significant and striking differences. We will also point out, along the way, how most of these differences are closely related to the basic, overriding difference we pointed out in Chapter Two, namely, that the Bible views God as both loving and judgmental, punishing sin in His wrath, while the Course views God as purely loving, devoid of any judgment or wrath.

THE CREATION OF THE WORLD

One of the most blatant differences between the Bible and the Course is their view of the creation of the world. This is often the first such difference that strikes the eye of a person who, familiar with the Bible, begins to study the Course.

The Bible: "In the beginning God created the heavens and the earth" (Gen. 1:1, NASB).

The Course: "Is it not strange that you believe to think you made the world you see is arrogance? God made it not. Of this you can be sure" (W-pI.152. 6:1-3).

In a nutshell, the Bible teaches that God created the world and pronounced it good. The Course teaches that the world was made by the mind of the Sonship, as a result of its mistaken belief in sin and separation.

The world was made as an attack on God....the world was meant to be a place where God could enter not, and where His Son could be apart from Him (W-pII.3.2:1, 4).

Some have questioned whether the Course actually means that God did not create the physical universe, contending that perhaps it means simply that God did not create the world *as we see it* through the eyes of fear. There are a number of places that refute that notion, perhaps the clearest, to me, being this:

> The world you see is an illusion of a world. God did not create it, for what He creates must be eternal as Himself. Yet there is nothing in the world you see that will endure forever. Some things will last in time a little while longer than others. But the time will come when all things visible will have an end (C-4.1:1-5).

No one would contend that the physical universe, nor any part of it, is eternal. "Some things" such as mountains, or planets, or stars, "will last in time a little while longer than others," but absolutely nothing in it is eternal. Therefore, the Course concludes, since God creates only things as "eternal as Himself," none of what we see ("all things visible") was created by God.

In the opinion of most Course interpreters, this view of the world's origin is fundamental to the metaphysical teaching of the Course, upon which its practical teaching of forgiveness is entirely based. It is connected, for instance, to the key difference we have already cited in Chapter Two: That God is a God of pure love, and not a god of vengeance. Many confused spiritual seekers have asked themselves, "How could a loving God have created a world like this, full of suffering, loss, pain, sickness and death?" Even if we take into account the Bible's story of the Fall, the post-Edenic world is still God's doing: He decreed that because of man's sin, man would now die, and would be forced to labor all the days of his life, fighting against the "thorns and thistles" of the world. Woman was cursed with multiplied pain in childbirth and subordination to her husband. How could a loving God do that? The Course's answer, in accord with its view of God as perfect Love, is quite simple: He didn't.

> For this world is the symbol of punishment, and all the laws that seem to govern it are the laws of death. Children are born into it through pain and in pain. Their growth is attended by suffering, and they learn of sorrow and separation and death. Their minds seem to be trapped in their brain, and its powers to decline if their bodies are hurt. They seem to love, yet they desert and are deserted. They appear to lose what they love, perhaps the most

insane belief of all. And their bodies wither and gasp and are laid in the ground, and are no more. Not one of them but has thought that God is cruel.

If this were the real world, God would be cruel. For no Father could subject His children to this as the price of salvation and be loving (T-13.in.2:4-3:2).

THE REALITY OF THE WORLD

The phrase mentioned in the last quotation, "the real world," points to another key difference between the Bible and the Course. Not only did God not create the world; the world is simply not real. This must be so because *only* that which is created by God is real:

God created nothing beside you and nothing beside you exists, for you are part of Him (T-10.In.2:1).

...everything that God created cannot have an end, and nothing He did not create is real (M-20.5:7).

Does that mean that we, as God's creations, cannot create anything real? No; but only what we create in alignment with His Will has any real existence:

...only what God creates or what you create with the same Will has any real existence (T-3.II.3:6).

The Bible simply presumes that the physical world is real; God created it, pronounced it good, and we now live in it. The Course unqualifiedly and emphatically states that the world does not even exist:

There is no world! This is the central thought the course attempts to teach (W-pI.132.6:2-3).

There is nothing outside you. That is what you must ultimately learn...(T-18.VI.1:1-2).

This is a very difficult idea for us to accept, as Lesson 132 goes on to explain. The world *seems* very real to us. The Course makes extensive use of the analogy of our dreams to explain how such a thing could be. It tells us that we know very well how in our dreams, we seem to be living in a completely real world, but that when we wake, we become aware the world we seemed to be part of actually existed nowhere but within our sleeping minds.

> You seem to waken, and the dream is gone. Yet what you fail to recognize is that what caused the dream has not gone with it. Your wish to make another world that is not real remains with you. And what you seem to waken to is but another form of this same world you see in dreams. All your time is spent in dreaming. Your sleeping and your waking dreams have different forms, and that is all (T-18.II.5:8-13).

In the Course's understanding, then, the world has no real existence; it "exists" only within our minds:

> Yet this world is only in the mind of its maker, along with his real salvation. Do not believe it is outside of yourself, for only by recognizing where it is will you gain control over it (T-12.III.9:8-9).

The unreality of the world is central to understanding how the Course can maintain that God is nothing but love, with no desire to punish us. Our sins do not merit punishment because, in reality, they never happened except in a dream. Our unloving thoughts literally have no real effects; they are mistakes, but not "sins."

> This world is causeless, as is every dream that anyone has dreamed within the world.…You may cause a dream, but never will you give it real effects (T-28.II.6:1, 5).

> …we rejoice to learn that we have made mistakes which have no real effects on us. Sin is impossible, and on this fact forgiveness rests upon a certain base more solid than the shadow world we see (W-pII.359.1:6-7).

The Course does indeed recognize that, although the effects of "sin" are not real, they are *real to us*, and therefore—at least temporarily— must be dealt with *as if* they were real, until we can truly come to accept their unreality.

> To condemn is thus impossible in truth. What seems to be its influence and its effects have not occurred at all. Yet must we deal with them a while as if they had (W-pI.198.2:5-7).

Thus, the Course meets us where we are, caught in believing in the reality of our dreams of a guilty world, and works with us on that basis with the ultimate aim of entirely liberating us from our illusions.

THE FALL

The phrase, "the Fall," does not actually occur in the Bible, but it has come into common use to describe mankind's abrupt descent from original grace into a sinful state. In *A Course in Miracles,* the phrase, "the separation," denotes a very similar concept, although it is viewed quite differently.

The Bible's picture of the Fall is best exemplified in the account given by Paul in the book of Romans:

> Because that, when they knew God, they glorified
> [him] not as God, neither were thankful; but became
> vain in their imaginations, and their foolish heart was
> darkened…And even as they did not like to retain God
> in [their] knowledge, God gave them over to a
> reprobate mind… (Rom. 1:21, 28, KJV).

Paul tells us that, "in Adam all die" (I Cor. 15:22, NASB). In other words, Adam's sin was transmitted to every succeeding generation. The Bible presents the story of Adam and Eve as an event in which man fell into sin, after which God condemned mankind to death, and banished him from His presence.

The Course, by contrast, tells us quite emphatically: "…the separation never occurred" (T-6.II.10:7). Just as the world has never really existed, so God's creation has never become separated from Him, not for an instant. The Course points out that once Adam fell asleep, we are never told he awoke (T-2.I.3:6); thus everything after that is merely a nightmare, not reality. Adam listened to the lies of the serpent, that is, to untruth (T-2.I.3:2); none of what followed was real. The belief that God rejected Adam and forced him from the Garden of Eden is called an error (T-3.I.3:9).

Our fundamental mistake was (and is) in believing that separation was even possible.

> You cannot walk the world apart from God, because
> you could not be without Him. He is what your life is.

> Where you are He is. There is one life. That life you share with
> Him. Nothing can be apart from Him and live (W-pI.156.2:4-9).

Here, too, we see the truth of God as Love. How could a loving God
have created a being that was even *capable* of separating from Him and
opposing His will? Again, the Course's answer is that a loving God could
not and did not do that.

> God does not suffer conflict. Nor is His creation split in two.
> How could it be His Son could be in hell, when God Himself
> established him in Heaven? Could he lose what the Eternal Will
> has given him to be his home forever? (W-pI.138.8:1-4)

THE QUESTION OF EVIL AND THE DEVIL

In the Bible, there is a consistent picture of two opposing forces, good
and evil, God and the devil. The Bible speaks of the devil as, "Your
adversary, the devil" who "prowls about like a roaring lion, seeking
someone to devour" (I Peter 5:8, NASB).

The Course utterly rejects the notion of a personal devil, a power
independent of God:

> The "devil" is a frightening concept because he seems to be
> extremely powerful and extremely active. He is perceived as a
> force in combat with God, battling Him for possession of His
> creations. The devil deceives by lies, and builds kingdoms in
> which everything is in direct opposition to God. Yet he attracts
> men rather than repels them, and they are willing to "sell" him
> their souls in return for gifts of no real worth. This makes
> absolutely no sense (T-3.VII.2:4-8).

Rather, the Course teaches, the "devil" is really a product of our own
minds: "The mind can make the belief in separation very real and very
fearful, and this belief *is* the 'devil'" (T-3.VII.5:1). Elsewhere the Course
tells us that, "The ego is the part of the mind that believes your existence is
defined by separation" (T-4.VII.1:5). Thus, the "devil" is the ego. Calling
upon the devil with psychic powers is actually, according to the Course, just
a way of calling on the ego, thus strengthening it (M-25.6:5).

According to the Course, "evil does not exist" (T-3.I.7:4). There is no
power opposing good, or God.

> What is the peace of God? No more than this; the simple

28

understanding that His Will is wholly without opposite. There is no thought that contradicts His Will, yet can be true (M-20.6:1-3).

The Course's thought system is monistic, while that of the Bible is consistently dualistic, two powers instead of only one. This core difference has profound effects on how the two books perceive man's problem, and the process of resolving that problem. One such effect, mentioned earlier, is that the Bible sees mankind, in the end, divided into two camps, one group going to Heaven, another to hell, according to their choice between good and evil. The Course, in great contrast, sees the salvation of all mankind as inevitable simply because there is no other alternative! "The acceptance of the Atonement by everyone is only a matter of time" (T-2.III.3:1).

If evil or the devil were real, then it would make some sense that God would need to be vengeful against evil and warlike against the devil, which is precisely why the Bible portrays God in that way. So here again we see that the overruling concept of God as only Love demands that evil and the devil be seen as nothing more than an illusion of our minds.

THE REALITY OF SIN

The Bible states:

For all have sinned and fall short of the glory of God (Rom. 3:23, NASB).

The Scripture has shut up all men under sin (Gal. 3:22, NASB).

There is none righteous, not even one (Rom 3:10, NASB, quoting Psalm 14:1).

The Course states: "There is no sin" (T-26.VII.10:5), and, "Son of God, you have not sinned, but you have been much mistaken" (T-10.V.6:1). Rather than asserting the guilt of all, it asserts their innocence:

But the content of the course never changes. Its central theme is always, "God's Son is guiltless, and in his innocence is his salvation" (M-1.3:4-5).

For the Bible, sin is real, and has caused a real breach between God and man. Sin is the fundamental problem, and the Bible's entire theology of redemption is based upon this belief in sin's reality. For the Course, sin is impossible: "To sin would be to violate reality, and to succeed" (T-19.II.2:2). Our only problem, then, is a mistake: an erroneous belief in sin and in separation from God as a result of sin. The Course's entire plan of salvation, then, is based on sin's illusory nature.

This denial of sin's reality stems from the Course's non-dualistic stance, discussed in the previous point. If there is no power opposed to God, and no will other than His, then how can sin be real? The Course is uncompromising on this point, and clearly sets itself in contrast to any belief system that holds to the reality of sin—which the Bible clearly does.

> A major tenet in the ego's insane religion is that sin is not error but truth, and it is innocence that would deceive. Purity is seen as arrogance, and the acceptance of the self as sinful is perceived as holiness. And it is this doctrine that replaces the reality of the Son of God as his Father created him, and willed that he be forever (T-19.II.4:1-3).

> The Son of God can be mistaken; he can deceive himself; he can even turn the power of his mind against himself. But he cannot sin (T-19.II.3:1-2).

> The Self which God created cannot sin (W-pII.330.1:5).

> There is no stone in all the ego's embattled citadel more heavily defended than the idea that sin is real; the natural expression of what the Son of God has made himself to be, and what he is (T-19.II.7:1).

I know from my own experience that, after twenty-three years of deep acceptance of the Bible's teaching, I had great difficulty in letting go of my belief in sin's reality. Although I had laid the Bible aside for six years before I discovered the Course, and had read widely in other religions, philosophies and psychologies, it took about three years of intensive study of the Course before I found myself able to consider that perhaps, on this point, the Course was right.

There is absolutely no way to reconcile the teaching of the Bible and the Course on this point. Either we have sinned, or we have not. Either we are innocent, or guilty. There is no in between. The Bible is just as emphatic on sin's reality as the Course is emphatic on its non-reality. Even John, the Apostle of Love, makes belief in our sinfulness a test of true Christian faith:

> If we say that we have no sin, we are deceiving ourselves, and the truth is not in us. If we confess our sins, He is faithful and righteous to forgive us our sins and to cleanse us from all unrighteousness. If we say that we have not sinned, we make

Him a liar, and His word is not in us (I John 1:8-10, NASB).

The difference in point of view on the issue of sin is glaring and stark; it cannot be explained away. If sin were real, it would demand punishment:

> There is nothing he [the Son of God] can do that would really
> change his reality in any way, nor make him really guilty. That
> is what sin would do, for such is its purpose. Yet for all the
> wild insanity inherent in the whole idea of sin, it is impossible.
> For the wages of sin is death, and how can the immortal die?
> (T-19.II.3:3-6)

The argument the Course presents here is the exact opposite of the Bible's way of thinking. The Bible says that since "the wages of sin is death" (Rom. 6:23, NASB), then since all men have sinned, all men must die. The Course accepts the premise that sin merits death, but it turns the argument around: Since God's Son is immortal, he cannot die; therefore sin must be impossible!

Our ruling principle—God is Love—goes hand in hand with the Course's refusal to accept sin as real. If sin were real, God would have to punish it; He would be (as the Bible presents Him) torn between His love and His sense of justice.

> If sin is real, God must be at war with Himself. He must be split,
> and torn between good and evil; partly sane and partially insane.
> For He must have created what wills to destroy Him, and has the
> power to do so. Is it not easier to believe that you have been
> mistaken than to believe in this? (T-19.III.6:3-6)

Believing in sin's reality is the root of our fear of God, our belief that He is other than totally loving.

THE NATURE OF JESUS

The New Testament teaches very clearly that Jesus was a unique being, "the only begotten God" (John 1:18, NASB), "the only begotten Son of God" (John 3:18, NASB). In Philippians, Paul teaches that Jesus "existed in the form of God," but "emptied himself...being made in the likeness of a man" (Phil. 2:5-7, NASB). Because of the work he performed in his manhood, "God highly exalted Him, and bestowed on Him the name which is above every name, that at the name of Jesus every knee should bow...and every tongue should confess that Jesus Christ is Lord..." (Phil 2:9-11, NASB). In other words, Jesus is God Himself in human form, the *only* such one, deserving of the worship of every other created being.

The Course, by contrast, teaches that "Jesus is the name of one who was a man but saw the face of Christ in all his brothers and remembered God. So he became identified with *Christ*, a man no longer, but at one with God" (C-5.2:1-2). "Jesus became what all of you must be" (C-5.3:1). Jesus was not God Who became man, but a man who remembered his own nature as Christ, God's Son, God's eternal creation. He was a man like we are, and what he became, we all must be. "Is he the Christ? Oh yes, along with you" (C-5.5:1-2).

The Course does agree that God has only one Son; in fact, it stresses that fact, but with a very different interpretation. Rather than identifying Jesus alone with that one Son, the Course insists that we are all part of the Son; together, we comprise "the Sonship."

> It should especially be noted that God has only one Son. If all His creations are His Sons, every one must be an integral part of the whole Sonship (T-2.VII.6:1-2).

Whereas the Bible teaching calls upon us all to bow our knees to Jesus as the God-man, in the Course Jesus, speaking in the first person, insists that we are his equals, and that he does not merit our worship:

> Equals should not be in awe of one another because awe implies inequality. It is therefore an inappropriate reaction to me. An elder brother is entitled to respect for his greater experience, and obedience for his greater wisdom. He is also entitled to love because he is a brother, and to devotion if he is devoted. It is only my devotion that entitles me to yours. There is nothing about me that you cannot attain. I have nothing that does not come from God. The difference between us now is that I have nothing else. This leaves me in a state which is only potential in you (T-1.II.3:5-13).

He adds that he is not "in any way separate or different from you except in time, and time does not really exist" (T-1.II.4:1).

In my opinion, the Bible's belief in the reality of sin and in God's need to punish it necessitated the elevation of Jesus from a mere man to God the Son. To somehow "pay for" the sins of all mankind, Jesus had to be seen as an infinite being capable of absorbing infinite punishment—the ultimate sacrifice. He had to be born of a virgin, free from the taint of inherited sin, in order to qualify as an unblemished sacrifice. "For he hath made him [to be] sin for us, who knew no sin; that we might be made the righteousness of God in him" (2 Co. 5:21, KJV).

Because the Course does not see God as punitive, nor sin as real, in its theology anyone could have begun the Atonement process of correcting our mistaken belief in separation. Jesus had no special advantage, nor did he need one. He just happened to be the first to fully complete his part in the Atonement process (C-6.2:2). This, and only this, qualifies him as our leader, deserving of our obedience.

THE MEANING OF THE CRUCIFIXION OF JESUS

The crucifixion of Jesus and its meaning is a core doctrine of Christianity. The Course teaches that the traditional interpretation found in the New Testament is, in a word, wrong. This is a difference with profound importance, so we will look at it quite carefully.

The Bible's teaching about the meaning of Jesus' death on the cross is that Jesus—the innocent, sinless God-man—died as a substitutionary sacrifice, taking the place of all mankind and bearing the sins of all for all time (which only an infinite Being could do), and suffered God's punishment of death in our place, so that we all could be set free from God's judgment on sin.

> He Himself [Jesus] bore our sins in His body on the cross, that we might die to sin and live to righteousness; for by His wounds you were healed (I Peter 2:24, NASB).

God's justice in punishing sin is upheld by the Bible as firmly as is His love. If sin is real, it must be punished, "For the wages of sin is death" (Rom 6:23, NASB). Yet if all have sinned, then all must die. How could a loving God let all His creations perish? Therefore, according to the Bible, He provided a way to be both "just and the justifier of the one who has faith in Jesus" (Rom. 3:26, NASB). He sent His only Son to become a sacrifice for our sins, "a propitiation in His blood through faith" (Rom. 3:25, NASB). "Christ died for our sins according to the Scriptures" (I Cor. 15:3, NASB). The prophecy of Isaiah concerning the "suffering servant," sung so beautifully as part of Handel's "Messiah," is applied in traditional Christian teaching to this sacrificial act of Jesus:

> Surely our griefs He Himself bore,
> And our sorrows He carried;
> Yet we ourselves esteemed Him stricken,

Smitten of God, and afflicted.
But He was pierced through for our transgressions,
He was crushed for our iniquities;
The chastening for our well-being fell upon Him,
And by His scourging we are healed.
All of us like sheep have gone astray,
Each of us has turned to his own way;
But the Lord has caused the iniquity of us all
To fall on Him (Isa. 53:4-6, NASB).

The Course directly and openly confronts this interpretation of Jesus' death and undertakes to correct it. In the first sections of Chapters 3 and 6 of the Text, the Course contradicts the biblical teaching and sets forth an entirely different view of what the crucifixion meant. It even offers some theories as to why the Bible contains what it sees as a gross misunderstanding of the event. Chapter 3 states what the crucifixion was *not*; Chapter 6 states what it *was*, the positive view.

In Chapter 3 the Course states:

> The crucifixion did not establish the Atonement; the resurrection did. Many sincere Christians have misunderstood this (T-3:I.1:2).

We might say "nearly all" in place of "many," because basing Atonement on the crucifixion has been the traditional teaching of the Christian church for most of its history. Jesus (for that is who is speaking in the Course) calls this "an upside-down point of view" (T-3.I.1:5), an "unfortunate interpretation, which arose out of projection," and an example of "anti-religious concepts" (T-3.I.1:5, 6, and 7). He asks: "Is it likely that God Himself would be capable of the kind of thinking which His Own words have clearly stated is unworthy of His Son?" (T-3.I.1:9)

He does not equivocate on the point; he tells us:

> It is so essential that all such thinking be dispelled that we must be sure that nothing of this kind remains in your mind. I was not "punished" because you were bad. The whole benign lesson the Atonement teaches is lost if it is tainted with this kind of distortion in any form (T-3.I.2:9-11).

He hammers this point home, in the process refuting the idea that God has any desire to punish sin or extract "vengeance" on mankind for their evil deeds:

God does not believe in retribution. His Mind does not create that way. He does not hold your "evil" deeds against you. Is it likely that He would hold them against me? Be very sure that you recognize how utterly impossible this assumption is, and how entirely it arises from projection (T-3.I.3:4-8).

In Chapter 6, he states that not only was the crucifixion not a form of punishment, but it also had a positive interpretation (T-6.I.1:3-5). He says it was "an extreme example" (T-6.I.2:1) that demonstrated "that it is not necessary to perceive any form of assault in persecution, because you cannot *be* persecuted" (T-6.I.4:6).

> I elected, for your sake and mine, to demonstrate that the most outrageous assault, as judged by the ego, does not matter. As the world judges these things, but not as God knows them, I was betrayed, abandoned, beaten, torn, and finally killed (T-6.I.9:1-2).

> I was persecuted as the world judges, and did not share this evaluation for myself. And because I did not share it, I did not strengthen it (T-6.I.5:3-4).

In other words, the crucifixion demonstrated that it is possible to perceive even the most extreme forms of seeming attack as something other than attack. By choosing not to share that perception (or "evaluation") of the events, Jesus taught that only love is real. He did not attack or judge in return. He tells us that, "The message of the crucifixion is perfectly clear: *Teach only love, for that is what you are*" (T-6.I.13:1).

How, then, did the understanding of the crucifixion come to be so distorted? The Course explains:

> The Apostles often misunderstood it, and for the same reason that anyone misunderstands it. Their own imperfect love made them vulnerable to projection, and out of their own fear they spoke of the "wrath of God" as His retaliatory weapon.... These are some of the examples of upside-down thinking in the New Testament, although its gospel is really only the message of love (T-6.I.14:2-3, 15:1).

In other words, the Apostles (and those who later wrote down their teachings) simply *misunderstood*. The teaching of the New Testament on this point, then, is clearly mistaken, in the opinion of the Course's author.

The paragraph last quoted above continues by giving several other examples of "upside-down thinking" in which Jesus claims that the Apostles misquoted him in the Bible, examples we have already examined in Chapter Two. He then returns to the general point:

> As you read the teachings of the Apostles, remember that I told them myself that there was much they would understand later, because they were not wholly ready to follow me at the time. I do not want you to allow any fear to enter into the thought system toward which I am guiding you. I do not call for martyrs but for teachers. No one is punished for sins, and the Sons of God are not sinners. Any concept of punishment involves the projection of blame, and reinforces the idea that blame is justified. The result is a lesson in blame, for all behavior teaches the beliefs that motivate it (T-6.I.16:1-6).

We will return to this passage later, since it gives clear instructions on how Course students should approach the Bible. For now, we note once again how the Course stresses that God is not a punitive deity, and negates any idea that we are sinful, or that anyone—Jesus or ourselves—is punished for sins.

MISCELLANEOUS DIFFERENCES

Without going into details, let me enumerate a few other significant differences between the Bible and the Course.

The Bible teaches a literal hell, with the wicked condemned to eternal torment. The Course says that hell is an idea we made up, brought on by our belief in guilt.

> There is no hell. Hell is only what the ego has made of the present (T-15.I.7:1-2).

The Bible's view of the Last Judgment is that God is meting out punishment to sinners; in the Course, it is the the Sons of God rejecting all their unloving thoughts (T-2.VIII.3-5).

The Bible sees the Second Coming of Christ as an event in which Jesus himself returns to Earth to separate the good from the bad (the sheep from the goats), and to rule in a literal kingdom. The Course sees it as the event in time when all minds are at last given to Christ, the true Self of all beings (W-pII.9.3:2).

The Bible says that the body is the temple of the Holy Spirit; the Course, while accepting that as a preliminary step, teaches that the true temple of the Holy Spirit is not a body but a relationship. Its view of the body, overall, is rather low; it refers to it as "a tiny spot of senseless mystery" (T-20.VI.5:1-2).

The Bible, in many ways, teaches the value of sacrifice; the Course teaches that "Sacrifice is a notion totally unknown to God" (T-3.I.4:1), and "you are never called on to sacrifice" (T-6.I.10:4).

The Bible teaches that Jesus is the Christ; the Course teaches that Christ is the Self we all share (W-pII.6.1:1-2).

The Bible teaches that Jesus taught us to remember him in communion by sharing his body and blood; the Course teaches that to share the body is to share nothing, and that true communion means sharing the *mind* of Christ, and seeing Christ in all our brothers (T-7.V.10:7-10; 11:2-6).

The Bible teaches that Heaven is the dwelling place of God, separate from Earth. The Course teaches that Heaven is here and now, and is simply "the awareness of perfect oneness" (M-24.6:4,6 and T-18.VI.1:6).

The Course sometimes says that certain Bible statements are in error. For instance, Jesus denies that he ever said, "I come not to bring peace but a sword," or "Betrayest thou the Son of Man with a kiss?" (to Judas); both statements are taken from the Gospels. In another example, the Course declares that the biblical statement, "The Word was made flesh" (John 1:14, KJV), is, strictly speaking, impossible, although it then proceeds to offer a very loose interpretation in which the idea is at least figuratively true: The Holy Spirit can use the body to give expression to the thoughts of God (T-8.VII.7).

Finally, the Bible—at least in the view of evangelical Christians and fundamentalists—teaches that its words are all inspired by God, and therefore without error ("All Scripture is inspired by God" [2 Tim. 3:16]; "the Scripture cannot be broken" [John 10:35]). Yet if, as we saw in the previous paragraph, the Course contends that the Bible contains statements which are attributed to Jesus, but which he never said, obviously it does not believe the Bible is without error! The many other disagreements the Course has with the Bible, and its references to the Bible's distortions and misunderstandings, makes it clear that the Course does not share the fundamentalist's view of the Bible's infallibility.

-FIVE-
Continuity

Despite its frequent disagreements with things in the Bible, the dominant essence of the Course's attitude towards the Bible is respect. More than just familiar with the Bible, the Course's author seems to approve of it, to count it as something important, and even to grant it a certain authority. The Course mentions the word "Bible" seventeen times, mostly in quoting it, and in nearly every one of these seventeen instances, it quotes it approvingly. Let's take a look at a few of these references, and see what they can tell us about how the Course views the Bible and itself as part of a single continuity of spiritual revelation.

HOW THE COURSE USES THE BIBLE

The direct references to the Bible generally fall into two groups: either they give simple approval to the Bible, or they approve what is said but offer a reinterpretation of the words.

Simple Approval
Sometimes, the Course seemingly quotes the Bible with simple approval, taking its statements at face value, and granting them the authority of truth.

> If you are afraid, you are valuing wrongly. Your understanding will then inevitably value wrongly, and by endowing all thoughts with equal power will inevitably destroy peace. That is why the Bible speaks of "the peace of God which passeth understanding." This peace is totally incapable of being shaken by errors of any kind (T-2.II.1:7-10).

In this case, the biblical phrase describing the peace of God is simply taken as valid. There is some amount of reinterpretation, because this passage is basically telling us that "passeth understanding" really means "incapable of being shaken by errors of any kind." Agreement, with an expanded understanding of the meaning. In a later passage referring to these same words, however, the Course limits their application only to the past, and asserts that, in the light of the real world it proclaims, peace *can* be understood:

> The peace of God passeth your understanding only in the past.
> Yet here it is and you can understand it now (T-13.VII.8:1-2).

It seems to be showing us, in this example, that the words of the Bible, although true, are sometimes true in only a limited sense.

There are a few instances where the Course does not bother reinterpreting the Bible at all; for instance:

> The Bible gives many references to the immeasurable gifts
> which are for you, but for which you must ask. This is not a
> condition as the ego sets conditions. It is the glorious condition
> of what you are (T-4.III.5:3-5).

The Course, in regard to the Bible, is saying little more here than, "The Bible is right." It says there are immeasurable gifts for you, and that you must ask for them, and that is true. It *does* go on to correct our usual understanding of that truth: Asking isn't a "condition" of receiving the gifts, something we have to do to earn them; rather, we must ask because our will is sovereign, and if we do not desire the gifts, we will not experience them. Nothing can be forced upon us. This correction, however, is not to what the Bible says, but to our misguided understanding of its truth.

Another very clear instance in which the Course approvingly quotes the Bible is this:

> The Bible says, "May the mind be in you that was also in Christ
> Jesus," and uses this as a blessing. It is the blessing of miracle-
> mindedness. It asks that you may think as I thought, joining with
> me in Christ thinking (T-5.I.3:4-6).

The meaning given the words by Jesus here is exactly the same as the original meaning in the Bible (see Phil. 2:2-5).

And again:

> The Bible emphasizes that all prayer is answered, and this is
> indeed true (T-9.II.3:1).

AGREEMENT WITH REINTERPRETATION

> The emptiness engendered by fear must be replaced by
> forgiveness. That is what the Bible means by "There is no
> death," and why I could demonstrate that death does not exist. I
> came to fulfill the law by reinterpreting it (T-1.IV.4:1-3).

The only specific Bible reference containing the words referred to here
is in the Old Testament book of Proverbs:

> In the way of righteousness [is] life; and [in] the pathway
> [thereof there is] no death (Pr. 12:28, KJV).

In the New Testament, there is a passage in I Corinthians 15 about the
resurrection of the body that proclaims:

> O death, where is your victory? O death, where is your sting?
> (I Cor. 15:55, KJV)

This, in turn, is a loose translation of Hosea 13:14 in the Old Testament.

In quoting these words, the Course seems, first of all, to simply agree
with them and approve of them. "There is no death." "Yes, that is so," the
author seems to be saying. What "no death" means, however, in terms of
the Course's teaching, is something besides physical immortality or a bodily
resurrection. "Death" is symbolic of "the emptiness engendered by fear;"
that emptiness will be replaced by forgiveness. Jesus is clearly
reinterpreting what the Bible said. He affirms its truth, and then gives the
words new meaning. He explains his actions by saying: "I came to fulfill
the law by reinterpreting it."

What is worthy of note is that Jesus is not *refuting* what the Bible said
here. He is not disagreeing with it or saying it was mistaken. He agrees, *and*
he reinterprets. He claims to be *fulfilling* the "law" (a term often generically
used in the New Testament to refer to the entire Old Testament). This
statement itself is a biblical allusion, for in the Gospel of Matthew, Jesus is
quoted as saying:

> Think not that I am come to destroy the law, or the prophets: I
> am not come to destroy, but to fulfil (Mt 5:17, KJV).

This attitude of Jesus in the Gospels towards the Old Testament is
strongly harmonious with Jesus' general attitude, in the Course, towards the
Bible as a whole. He is not destroying it, or negating it; he considers
himself to be fulfilling it, that is, to be completing it. There is a strong

flavor of *continuity* here; Jesus is implying that in the biblical words quoted, there is a germ of truth, and that now he is elaborating on what that truth really is.

Another reference to the Old Testament in the Course is: "Yet the Bible says that a deep sleep fell upon Adam, and nowhere is there reference to his waking up" (T-2.I.3:6). Once again, the basic Bible statement is simply taken at face value, as valid: "a deep sleep fell upon Adam" (referring to Gen. 2:21). Then, it is given new meaning: *nowhere does it say he woke up.* In the next sentence, the Course applies this notion to the whole course of human history: "The world has not yet experienced any comprehensive reawakening or rebirth;" in other words, we are still asleep. Once again we get a sense of continuity of truth, hidden or perhaps garbled in the Bible, but now fully explained.

Another example:

> Because their hearts are pure, the innocent defend true
> perception instead of defending themselves against it.
> Understanding the lesson of the Atonement they are without the
> wish to attack, and therefore they see truly. This is what the
> Bible means when it says, "When he shall appear (or be
> perceived) we shall be like him, for we shall see him as he is"
> (T-3.II.5:8-10).

Here, too, we see no negation of what the Bible says, but a reinterpretation of what the words actually mean. Traditionally this New Testament statement (I John 3:2) has been understood by Christians to refer to the reappearance of Jesus in the world at the Second Coming, at which time we will be suddenly "translated" into his likeness, receiving "spiritual bodies" like his (see also I Cor. 15:52-54). The Course gives it a completely different spin: When we see with true perception, perceiving the pure Son of God in all of God's creation, we shall be like Jesus.

In this case, I think it is worth pointing out again that there is good reason to doubt that the meaning given to these words by Jesus is actually the meaning that was in the mind of the biblical author who wrote them! That is, Jesus is reinterpreting them in a way that the human author probably did not intend. And yet, the way that the Course so often strives to find ways to make the words of the Bible acceptable seems, to me, an attempt to forge a sense of continuity between the two books, a desire to see them as somehow in harmony and complimentary to one another.

One more example should make the point quite clear:

> When the Bible says "Judge not that ye be not judged," it means
> that if you judge the reality of others you will be unable to avoid
> judging your own (T-3.VI.1:4).

By now you should be able to see the same two elements here:
agreement and reinterpretation. The usual understanding of these words
down through the years has been, "Don't judge others or God will judge
you." The Course makes them mean, "Don't judge others or you will
inevitably judge yourself." In this case, the original words could be
understood either way. They are taken from Jesus' "Sermon on the Mount"
in Matthew 7:1, and quite possibly, when Jesus originally uttered them,
were meant to be understood exactly as he interprets them here.

I conclude from the way the Course uses the Bible, of which I have given
only a few selected examples, that it assumes a distinct and rather clear
continuity between the Bible and its own teachings. It views itself as in the
same lineage of teaching as the Bible. The Course does not see itself as refuting
or negating what the Bible says; rather, it takes the Bible's words as a valid
starting point, and offers new interpretations of them. The Course in no way
attempts to destroy the Bible's message; instead, it sees itself as the fulfillment
or completion of the Bible.

THE ROLE OF JESUS AS TEACHER IN THE BOOKS

Another obvious point of continuity between the books is the role of
Jesus as the primary teacher in both the New Testament and the Course.
This continuity in regard to Jesus does not exist with the Old Testament,
naturally; the New Testament shows continuity with the Old in other ways,
which we will look at in more detail in Chapter Seven.

I have already referred, in Chapter Four, to the comments of Jesus in the
Course about how his disciples, who wrote most of the New Testament, had
misunderstood the message of the crucifixion and misreported some of his
sayings. It is worth noting that he does not disavow these people; he still
recognizes them as his followers. The situation we have, then, is that of the
same spiritual teacher in both books. He identifies himself as the one whose
life and words are reported upon in the Bible. He acknowledges those who
wrote the Bible as his followers. But, in the Course, he is correcting their
mistakes and misunderstandings.

The New Testament, then, in Jesus' own understanding, grew out of his
own teachings, but presented them through the distorted lens of the
disciples' own "imperfect love" and "fear" (T-6.I.14:3). What is even more

relevant to us in determining our own attitude towards the Bible is that Jesus seems to assume that some of us, at least, will want to read the New Testament! He says, "As you read the teachings of the Apostles, remember that I told them myself that there was much they would understand later" (T-6.I.16:1). The words, "As you read...," clearly assume that we will be reading those writings. There is certainly no indication that he dismisses the Bible as worthless, discouraging us from reading the Bible because it is "all of the ego."

Some Course teachers (in particular Kenneth Wapnick, in his book, *Absence From Felicity*) make the assumption that Jesus' evident approval of the Bible, and his quotation of certain Bible passages as being his own words, were somehow nothing more than accommodations to Helen Schucman's belief that the Bible contained his teaching, at least partially. These words, "As you read...," might then be referring simply to *Helen's* reading of the Bible. However, in the Course itself, there are no grounds for such an interpretation. The line, "As you read the teachings of the Apostles...," seems as worthy of universal application as is the opening line of the preceding paragraph in the Text, "If you interpret the crucifixion in any other way..." (T-6.I.14:1).

One can easily surmise from Jesus' statement that the "much they would understand later" is, in fact, the Course itself—a continuation and completion of what was begun two thousand years ago. In the Course, speaking of himself in the third person while clarifying the meaning of the terms "Jesus" and "Christ," Jesus says that his life on earth was not sufficient to complete his task:

> His little life on earth was not enough to teach the mighty lesson
> that he learned for all of you. He will remain with you to lead
> you from the hell you made to God (C-5.5:3-4).

Jesus "remains" with us, certainly, in spirit, for he offers (in the Course) to be our teacher and personal guide, and to help us deal with the scraps of fear within our minds if we bring them to him (T-4.III.7). Yet the Course itself, certainly, is one way in which he has chosen, while remaining with us, to lead us from the hell we have made to God. This, to me, shows that there is an intended continuity between his earthly ministry (which we know only from the Bible) and the Course.

In the Course, Jesus frequently uses the words, "I came," in various contexts. These frequent repetitions are obviously references to his appearance in the world, the life he lived in Galilee, the story of which is told in the

Gospels. In these passages, Jesus clearly is saying that his physical appearance in the world was part of the same process of revelation which is now continued in *A Course in Miracles*. For instance:

> You were in darkness until God's Will was done completely
> by any part of the Sonship. When this was done, it was perfectly
> accomplished by all. How else could it be perfectly
> accomplished? My mission was simply to unite the will of the
> Sonship with the Will of the Father by being aware of the
> Father's Will myself. This is the awareness I came to give you,
> and your problem in accepting it is the problem of this world
> (T-8.IV.3:1-5).

Jesus speaks of his "mission" in the past tense; he lived to perfectly accomplish God's Will, and when that was done by one (Jesus) it was accomplished by all. He says he "came" (past tense, referring to his life on earth) to give us this awareness, and that our "problem in accepting it" (present tense, for we who read his teachings in the Course now) "is the problem of this world." Clearly then, his present work in the Course is a continuation of his past work while on earth.

> When I said "I am come as a light into the world," I meant that I
> came to share the light with you (T-5.VI.11:1).

The statement is a quotation from John 12:46, a statement made during his life on earth; the purpose of that life was to share the light with us. In the Course, he then identifies himself with that same purpose, telling us not to look into "the ego's dark glass" (T-5.VI.11:2).

> God's Sons are equal in will, all being the Will of their Father.
> This is the only lesson I came to teach (T-8.IV.6:8-9).

In the context of this statement, the lesson of the paragraph leading up to these words is that God gave our will its power, and nothing created can oppose it. This was true of Jesus, which he demonstrated during his life on earth, and it is true of all God's Sons: "God's Sons are equal in will." Jesus then says that this was the same lesson he was teaching during his earthly life. His life was intended to establish what was possible for all of us, and the Course is continuing that same teaching.

Finally, the following quotation states decisively that the lesson Jesus was "born to teach" is the same lesson he "still would teach." For me, this establishes that the message he taught then, which is reported in the New

Testament (although unclearly and with much admixture of ego-based thoughts), is not reversed in the Course, but continued and clarified.

> The lesson I was born to teach, and still would teach to all my brothers, is that sacrifice is nowhere and love is everywhere (T-15.XI.7:5).

-SIX-
Qualified Supersession

The Course presents itself as the successor to the Bible and its teachings, but in a qualified way. This final point I want to make about how the Course actually views the Bible has already been brought out several times as we discussed various passages in which the concept was clearly indicated. I simply want to focus on it and underscore it in this chapter.

I call this idea "qualified supersession" (with thanks to Robert Perry, who gave me those words) because, although the Course sees itself quite clearly as superseding the Bible, it does so with certain qualifications. When I say the Course *supersedes* the Bible, I mean that it presents itself as the higher authority; in case of conflict, the teaching of the Course takes precedence.

The Course does not attempt, however, to *reject* the Bible; rather, it takes what the Bible has to say and acknowledges the truth it contains and the pure revelation which inspired it. But it also proceeds further, to explain distortions and misunderstandings in the Bible, to correct its errors, and to reinterpret many of its statements, giving them a higher (and often very different) meaning. It supersedes in that it strips away all the husk of ego distortions, but yet it retains and honors the germ of truth within.

This understanding, with some examples, will form the basis for a theory of *progressive revelation*, which I will describe in the following chapter. Let us first, then, briefly review a few of the ways in which the Course clearly presents itself as the Bible's successor, superseding its teachings.

THE COURSE AS SUCCESSOR TO THE BIBLE

Corrections to Biblical Teachings

We have already seen a number of ways in which the Course speaks in a way that supersedes the Bible. Chapter Four, on the differences between the two books, is comprised entirely of examples in which the Course presents itself as having authority to correct the Bible.

Redefinition of Biblical Terms

We've also seen several examples of the way the Course uses Bible terms, but infuses them with a newer and higher meaning; terms such as "Christ" and "Atonement," for instance. With an assumption of higher authority, the Course now comes along to tell us, "This is what the Bible meant when it said...."

Assumption of the Bible's Imperfection

In offering its corrections, the Course assumes that the Bible has errors, "upside-down thinking," and incorrect quotations of Jesus' words. To stand thus in judgment on the Bible, once again, assumes that the Course is in a position of having a higher authority.

QUALIFICATIONS TO SUPERSESSION

In contrast to these claims to higher authority, qualifying them somewhat, are the strong points of agreement between the two books, and the obvious continuity of teaching discussed in the last chapter. The word "supersede" by itself carries the meaning, "to set aside as void, useless, or obsolete." For example, if the 55 MPH speed limit is superseded by a new law setting the speed limit at 75 MPH on Interstate highways, the old law becomes useless and obsolete.

The Course does not supersede the Bible in that absolute manner. It does not render the Bible "void, useless or obsolete." The very fact that the Course quotes or alludes to the Bible 881 times demonstrates that it does not consider the Bible useless. Not all of the Bible's teachings are seen as mistaken; many are taken up by the Course and affirmed. The relationship of the Course to the Bible is much more like an amendment to the Constitution than it is like one law that completely replaces another. The kernel of the old meaning still stands, but now has been amended—clarified, explained differently, corrected in certain aspects, enhanced and refined to a higher level.

HOW VALID IS THE COURSE'S CLAIM TO AUTHORITY?

This question could be debated endlessly. There is no way that anyone can prove the Course has greater authority than the Bible. Certainly, anyone who believes the Bible is God's final message to mankind will reject out of hand such a claim as unworthy of any consideration. To fundamentalist Christians, the Course is heretical, and the proof is simply that it can be shown to contradict the Bible; in fact, several Christian books about cults and heresies include sections about *A Course in Miracles.*

To me, the proof of the Course's higher authority lies in my own experience as a result of studying it and practicing its teachings. I thank God that, despite my entrenched belief in the Bible, eleven and a half years ago I had enough openness of mind to overlook, for the time being, the troubling way the Course attempted to correct the Bible, which in my opinion was arrogance. I read it anyhow for the things I could agree with, the things I found helpful. Those fragments of Course teaching turned out to be more effective in bringing me peace of mind and happiness than the entire Bible had ever been. I saw miracles happening in my life, and in the lives of those around me. Those experiences with the Course opened my mind to question my fundamental assumptions about the Bible's complete reliability.

"Proof by personal experience" is the method of validation that the Course itself recommends! It says:

> This course offers a very direct and a very simple learning situation, and provides the Guide Who tells you what to do. If you do it, you will see that it works. Its results are more convincing than its words. They will convince you that the words are true (T-9.V.9:1-4).

If you find yourself questioning which has the higher authority, the Bible or the Course, nothing I say to you is going to convince you one way or the other. Indeed, nothing that the Course itself says will convince you of its authority, a fact the Course acknowledges in the passage just quoted. What can convince you? Only your own experience. "If you do it [what the Course, and its Guide—the Holy Spirit—tell you to do], you will see that it works." That is what convinced me, and that is the only thing that can convince you.

Lesson 327 in the Workbook reiterates this same idea. There, we are urged to consider God's promises and to "try them" and "test them." It asserts that if we do so, we will learn from our experience that they are true, and that faith will surely follow.

-SEVEN-

A Coherent Approach to the Bible

We've seen that the Course displays several different aspects in relationship with the Bible. It shows us:

- Similarities
- Differences
- Continuity
- Qualified Supersession

It teaches many of the same truths. It differs significantly on many points. It seems to continue the mission of the Bible in some way, and yet at the same time, to supersede it, laying claim to a higher authority.

How can we put this all together into some coherent understanding of the relationship between the two books? I have chosen to call my attempt to do so *a theory of progressive revelation*. I have been aided in this attempt by the fact that I had already faced an identical problem in the past, as a Bible student, in trying to understand the relationship between the Old and New Testaments. That relationship can, I believe, be very instructive to us in understanding how the Course, in its turn, relates to those earlier forms of God's revelation to man.

THE RELATIONSHIP OF THE OLD AND NEW TESTAMENTS

If you know the Bible somewhat, you will easily realize that the same points we have made about the Course and the Bible are also true of these two parts of the Bible. In some ways they are very similar, yet in many points they clearly differ. There is a definite continuity between the two books. And quite clearly, the New Testament presents itself as having a higher authority, sufficient to correct and reinterpret certain things that are in the Old Testament.

The New Testament Redefines Old Testament Terms

The Old Testament, for instance, centered around the nation of Israel. Israel was the Kingdom of God on Earth. The Kingdom of God was a political Kingdom. Jesus, inaugurating the New Testament era, came proclaiming that the Kingdom of God was within us, and that it was "not of this world" (Luke 17:20; John 18:36, NASB). It took the Apostle Paul to realize the full implications of this and to begin carrying the message of the Gospel to non-Jews. The way in which Jesus took up the same term, "Kingdom of God," used in the Old Testament, and yet redefined it and infused it with new meaning is exactly like what Jesus does in the Course with so many other biblical terms.

Jesus Corrected and Expanded on the Old Testament

Jesus, in the Gospels, assumed a higher authority than the Old Testament, and openly corrected what he saw as limited or incorrect understandings expressed there. He referred to a commandment of God recorded in Leviticus 19:17-18, in which the obligation of love was limited to one's countrymen, and then added, "But I say to you, love your enemies, and pray for those who persecute you" (Matt. 5:44, NASB). He incorporated the commandment to love one's neighbor but then *expanded* it to include even one's enemies.

The Sermon on the Mount in Matthew is filled with recurrences of the phrases, "You have heard" and "But I say to you" (see Matt. 5:21-22, 27-28, 33-34, 38-39), each of them an instance in which Jesus dares to make his own words supersede those from the Old Testament.

Revelation of Old Testament Limited by Its Hearers

Another time Jesus was discussing the provisions for divorce in the law of Moses: that a man could write a certificate of divorce and send away his wife. He said, "Because of your hardness of heart he wrote you this commandment" (Mark 10:5, NASB). In the parallel account in Matthew, he says that divorce is proper only for grounds of adultery, adding that "Not all men can accept this statement, but only those to whom it has been given" (Matt. 19:8-11, NASB).

My purpose here is not to discuss the validity of divorce—that can be a thorny topic! My interest is in those words, "Because of the hardness of your heart he wrote you this commandment." What do they tell us about the Old Testament scriptures? They clearly imply that the specific form of the message being given was adjusted to the level of receptivity in the hearers. They were given only as much as they could accept at the time. We might say that the truth was toned down for them, because if given in its highest form, they would simply have rejected it.

Bear in mind that, prior to the laws given by Moses, no certificate of divorce was required at all. Women were chattel. A man who tired of his wife could simply put her out of his house, with no legal standing. The certificate of divorce was a major step upwards for women, because it granted a legal standing to a divorced woman, freeing her from her marriage to the man who no longer wanted her, and allowing her to seek another marriage. True, it was a long way from today's equal property rights, alimony and child support. But it was a significant improvement over previous conditions.

Ken Wapnick's book, *Love Does Not Condemn,* contains an interesting short remark by Jesus from otherwise unpublished material that confirms this idea of revelation being adjusted to the hearers:

> I told you before that the word "thirst" in connection with the
> Spirit was used in the Bible because of the limited understanding
> of those to whom I spoke. I also told you not to use it (*Love
> Does Not Condemn*, pg. 483).

Clearly Jesus is saying that the understanding of the hearers affected the form revelation took in the Bible, and even constrained it into an imperfect form. He also implies ("I told you not to use it") that the Course is addressed to people whose understanding is not quite as limited as those who lived 2000 years ago, and therefore is taking a purer form.

Revelation Can Be Misunderstood by Its Hearers

Besides the concept that the revelation was *deliberately* toned down to match the level of those who heard it, there is also the idea that the revelation was given clearly, but was misunderstood. We've seen how Jesus says that the New Testament writers misunderstood his message, particularly his crucifixion. Another interesting example occurs in the personal messages from Jesus to Helen Schucman that were published in Wapnick's *Absence From Felicity.*

There, Jesus was talking to Helen about her superstitious fear of using people's real names in her writing (she often referred to her husband, Louis, by the name of Jonathan, for instance). He then says:

> Actually, the Jewish superstition about changing names was a
> distortion of a Revelation about how to alter or avert death. What
> the Revelation's proper content was, was that those "who change
> their mind" (not name) about destruction (or hate) do not need to
> die (*Absence from Felicity*, pg. 241).

53

Thus, here we have Jesus supporting the notion that human instruments can hear a true revelation, and misunderstand or misapply it quite drastically. They can distort the revelation to the point where it seems to become something entirely different—in this case, a teaching about changing *the mind* became a superstition about changing *names*. This is a key principle in understanding how the Course reinterprets the Bible. Often, its reinterpretation seems completely different from what was obviously the intent of the human author, as we have seen in several cases.

Just a few sentences later, in material that was later included in the Course, Jesus applies this principle to the Law (i.e. the Old Testament): "The law itself, if properly understood, offers only protection. It is those who have not yet changed their minds who brought the 'hell-fire' concept into it" (T-1.IV.4:4-5). This implies that the Law was itself a distorted revelation that now needs to be reinterpreted in a way that reconnects with the original content of the revelation. This indicates that the Course's author believes that the *original revelation* that inspired the Bible, even the Old Testament, was correct and true, but that the human authors often distorted that revelation and even completely misunderstood it, so that what was written down may be far from the original revelation. Nevertheless, with the assistance of the Holy Spirit, it is still possible to recover the original intent behind the garbled words.

New Testament Teaching is a Higher Revelation

The same indications of partial or limited revelation show up in other ways Jesus corrected the Old Testament. He pointed out that while the Old Testament advocated the concept of "an eye for an eye," the higher stance was to turn the other cheek. Once again, the idea of equal retribution was a major step upwards from the prevailing conditions of the time of Moses, for as the stories in the Old Testament record, the earlier practice was that if someone did something like rape your sister, the accepted response was to get your family together to annihilate the entire family of the offender. "An eye for an eye" mitigated the evil of attack without entirely removing it, because the people of that time were incapable of receiving such a radical teaching as turning the other cheek.

The full truth was nonviolence, non-attack. Limiting retribution to the level of the crime was only a beginning step in that direction. Over the millennia, the way that the truth about non-attack came through in revelation shows a progressive understanding, an increasing openness to accept the full implications of God's true desire for men in such situations.

In relationship to the New Testament, then, the Old was a limited and imperfect revelation. It was the truth for its time, but now (in Jesus' day) a new time had come. A higher understanding was possible. The *same truth* was being spoken, but the capacity of men to receive that truth had grown to the point where it could be stated more clearly and more completely.

Older Revelation Honored by the Newer

And yet, the new did not utterly reject the old. The old was honored and respected as having served a valid purpose—in its time. Paul, in speaking of "the Law," which refers to the entire Law of Moses with all its rules and regulations, says it "was added because of transgressions" (Gal. 3:19, NASB)—the same idea as the certificate of divorce having been decreed because of the hardness of men's hearts. It was a necessary but intermediate step, sort of a holding action on God's part. The Law "kept in custody" (Gal. 3:23, NASB) God's people; it protected them until they were ready for something more.

> The Law has become our tutor to lead us to Christ, that we may
> be justified by faith. But now that faith has come, we are no
> longer under a tutor (Gal. 3:24-25, NASB).

The Law served a positive purpose. It was a good thing. It was God's revelation—but it was not the full truth! And now, in the New Testament era, a fuller truth had come, and superseded the old revelation. It did not invalidate the old revelation; it completed it. The old *led to* the new, just as a tutor leads his pupils to the point of independence from his own teaching.

The very names of the two major divisions of the Bible are indicative of their relationship. "Testament" means a *covenant* or agreement, in this case, an agreement between God and man. And the "new" agreement obviously supersedes the "old" one. Yet all through the New Testament, a great reverence is displayed for the older writings. Although they are superseded now, they are seen as having led up to the new revelation. They even *predicted* that a higher teaching would come, and a "new covenant" would be made. For instance, the New Testament book of Hebrews, which is all about the ways in which the new covenant supersedes the old one, approvingly quotes from the Old Testament prophecy of Jeremiah, in which he wrote, "Behold, days are coming, says the Lord, when I will effect a new covenant..." (Heb. 8:8-12, Jer. 31:31-34, NASB).

Thus we see that revelation from God came in stages, with a higher revelation coming along with greater authority and clearer teaching. The

New Testament completely replaced some provisions of the Old Testament, such as animal sacrifices and acceptance with God based on obedience to laws. It replaced such things with the mystical, universal sacrifice of Jesus' crucifixion, and acceptance with God based on grace, through faith. The new was not, however, a rejection of the old; it was a higher form of it.

THE COURSE AS CONTINUING PROGRESSIVE REVELATION

Perhaps you can see where I am heading with all of this talk about the Old and New Testaments. I see the Course standing in relationship to the New Testament almost exactly as the New Testament stands in relationship to the Old. It is a higher, more complete understanding of God's unchanging revelation. It is presenting the same content (the same original revelation from God) in a purer manifestation. In some ways, the new form presented in the Course seems to be a radical change from what the New Testament teaches; it seems to completely contradict that teaching. But in reality, it does not contradict; it fulfills, it uplifts, it augments. It is a more perfect *reception* of the same truths God has always been trying to impart to us.

When the New Testament teachers declared that Jesus' single sacrifice had rendered any lesser sacrifices unnecessary, completely loosing mankind from all penalty for sin for all time, it was a change no less radical than the one the Course now makes in declaring that no sacrifice at all is needed, because no sin has actually occurred. The discerning reader can see a definite continuity in this progression of teaching, a movement from a lesser understanding to a greater. The new teaching does not make the old teaching wrong; it is simply more complete.

There is a story of four blind monks who encounter an elephant. Each approaches the elephant and grasps a particular part: one the trunk, one a leg, one the tail, and one the elephant's huge abdomen. And each reports on what an elephant feels like:

"An elephant is like a snake." "An elephant is like a tree." "An elephant is like a rope." "An elephant is like a wall."

Were any of the monks "wrong?" No; according to what they had experienced of the elephant, they were all correct. But all of their understandings were incomplete.

The Bible is an imperfect reception of the revelation of God's nature, and the way He interacts with mankind. The revelation that inspired it was correct, but men's egos "mis-received" it and distorted it to some degree. If we accept what the Course is saying, *A Course in Miracles* is a more complete understanding, a purer expression of the same truth about the same God. Therefore, just as the Apostles did not need to totally invalidate the Old Testament in order to proclaim their new understanding, neither do we, as Course students, need to invalidate the Bible in order to hold to the higher understanding the Course presents. The Bible and its teachings are part of what got us here, part of what prepared us for the Course, just as the Law acted as a tutor, keeping mankind in custody until the later revelation could come through.

SOME EXAMPLES OF PROGRESSIVE REVELATION

In closing this chapter, I think it will be helpful, in order to make the concept of progressive revelation less abstract and more concrete, to look at two specific examples of such progression, from the Old Testament, to the New, and finally, to the Course.

Loving Our Enemies

We have already seen how Jesus in the Gospels extended the Old Testament teaching about loving our neighbors (our countrymen) to a larger and broader teaching about loving our enemies. Elsewhere, in the Parable of the Good Samaritan (Luke 10:25-37), he also expanded our understanding of what "neighbor" meant (see verses 36 and 37); although a Samaritan was despised by most Israelites—not a "countryman"—he was identified as the true "neighbor" in the story.

The same teaching is raised to an even higher level in the Course material. In the Song of Prayer pamphlet, Jesus refers to his own earlier teaching about loving and praying for our enemies, and goes beyond it. In S-1.II.4-5, he teaches that, from a higher point of view, we have no enemies. He tells us that a deeper interpretation of praying for our enemies is that we need to pray for ourselves, that our minds would be changed from their perception of enemies, enabling us to recognize Christ in everyone and see their sinlessness.

Here we see the progression: from attacking our enemies, to praying for them, to realizing that there is no such thing as an enemy!

The Way Out of Guilt

The Law of the Old Testament provided a way for men to handle guilt, and to escape the consequences of their sins, through animal sacrifices, the annual Day of Atonement, and diligent obedience to God's laws. The New

Testament expanded that by presenting a way, through faith in Christ, to become entirely free of condemnation and guilt once and for all. The Course now informs us that sin and guilt are simply illusions made up by our own minds. In all three cases, the content is release from guilt and union with God, but in each progressive revelation, the release and union are more complete, and the method easier to grasp.

SUMMARY

Thus, in my opinion, the best way to see the relationship between the Course and the Bible is to understand the Course as the next major step in revelation after the Bible. It is grounded in the Bible, it takes up the truths the Bible was trying to impart to us, but it presents them in a higher form. Some have said the Course might be thought of as "The Third Testament," and that is, in my mind, a title the Course merits, although I believe the Course can stand by itself, apart from the Bible, much more easily than the New Testament could stand apart from the Old.

Is the Course the Final Revelation?

One final thought: The idea of progressive revelation may raise a question in our minds. Is the Course the final revelation? Is its truth the highest possible form of truth? Or can something higher come along?

In brief, I would say the answers are "probably not," "definitely not," and "probably so."

Before you race out to buy the successor to the Course, however, think a little about the time perspective here. Conservative Bible scholars place the Exodus (which led to the Law of Moses being formulated and written down, starting with Genesis) at approximately 1490 BC. Jesus inaugurated the New Testament era, and the Course came along about 1980 years later, assuming the accuracy of current estimates that Jesus was born in 4 BC, not in Year 1 AD. So we have about 1500 years between the beginnings of the first and second Testaments, and nearly 2000 years between the second and the third (the Course). Given that time scale I think it is extremely unlikely any of us will see something that supersedes the Course in our lifetimes. In my opinion, the books I have seen so far that purport to go beyond the Course in some way, or even to correct its "errors," are puny and powerless in comparison to the Course itself.

My own belief is that nothing higher than the Course is likely to show up until the Course has been as completely accepted and applied as is humanly possible, taking into account our own "hardness of heart" and reluctance to receive what it is saying. The Course has only been around for twenty-one years; its work, and its acceptance, has barely begun. There may come a day, hundreds or thousands of years from now, when mankind's consciousness has been raised to a sufficiently higher level such that an even more perfect revelation can be given—if it is still needed at that time. Who can say? I believe, based on statements in the Course itself, that its teaching, if fully applied, can take us all the way to the real world, just outside the gates of Heaven. Perhaps we won't absorb it completely enough; perhaps our resistance will insist on diluting it and misunderstanding it, so that a new revelation will be needed. Yet it is equally possible—and perhaps more likely, given the sure help of the Holy Spirit—that men and women will arise who embody the Course and exemplify it, who become a living testament to its truths, and living manifestations of the Holy Spirit in the world. In such a case, additional written revelation might be superfluous.

-EIGHT-
The Bible and Course Students

In this final chapter, we'll take a look at three questions: Should Course students read the Bible? If so, why should we? If we read the Bible, how should we interpret it? My answers to these questions will be based partly on what we have seen about the way the Course regards the Bible, and partly on my own thoughts and experience.

SHOULD COURSE STUDENTS READ THE BIBLE?

My answer, in brief, is that reading the Bible can be useful to Course students, but it is not *necessary*.

On the one hand, there is no necessity for any student of the Course to study the Bible, nor even read it. The Course is very clear that it views itself as complete and sufficient for our spiritual study, and that nothing outside the Course is necessary: "...you are studying a unified thought system in which nothing is lacking that is needed, and nothing is included that is contradictory or irrelevant" (W-pI.42.7:2). If that statement is true, that the Course lacks nothing that is needed, there cannot possibly be anything in the Bible that Course students *need*.

On the other hand, I believe that most Course students could benefit, at some time, from making an effort to at least become familiar with the Bible. Just because the Course contains everything that is *needed* does not mean it contains *everything*. There are many things outside the Course that can be helpful and useful for Course students, and the Bible is right up there at the top of that list.

So, with that clarification behind us, let's take a look at some of the reasons why students of the Course may find reading the Bible to be beneficial.

WHY SHOULD WE READ THE BIBLE?

Jesus Quotes It So Often in the Course

If Jesus thought enough of the Bible to refer to it nearly nine hundred times in the Course, surely that gives us some reason to read the Bible itself, even if for no other reason than to find out what the mistakes are that the Course is correcting. Obviously, the author of the Course believes that there is much in the Bible that is of interest to his readers, and that can be useful to them.

As Background for Understanding the Course

So many of the Course's symbols and metaphors are based on the Bible that reading the Bible, and understanding the original usage of those symbols or the stories referred to by the Course, can only augment our understanding of what the Course is saying.

For instance, the Course, several times, talks about the Son of God "arising" and returning to his "Father's House." To someone familiar with the Bible these seem like obvious references to the parable of The Prodigal Son (Luke 15:11-32). As an example, Workbook Lesson 193 contains these words: "For now we would arise in haste and go unto our Father's house" (W-pI.193.11:2). If you know the story of the Prodigal Son, those words take on a rich emotional content that is entirely lacking if you are not familiar with the story.

Jesus, in fact, actually *assumes* familiarity with the story in Chapter 8. He does summarize it, but knowing the entire story as told in the Bible can only increase the student's understanding as the Course explains the story's meaning:

> Listen to the story of the prodigal son, and learn what God's treasure is and yours: This son of a loving father left his home and thought he had squandered everything for nothing of any value, although he had not understood its worthlessness at the time. He was ashamed to return to his father, because he thought he had hurt him. Yet when he came home the father welcomed him with joy, because the son himself was his father's treasure. He wanted nothing else (T-8.VI.4).

For a Better Understanding of Jesus

When you become particularly interested in a certain author, leader, political figure, or spiritual teacher, you will often want to read his biography. The biography of Jesus, as a man, is the Gospels, in the Bible. While I do not assert that every word of these stories is one hundred percent historically accurate, there is no question that reading them gives us a picture of Jesus as a man that nothing else can do.

Helen Was Urged to Read the Bible

Helen Schucman was urged, through the guidance of Jesus she recorded, to read the Bible. He told her:

> You have every right to examine my credentials—in fact, I urge you to do so. You haven't read the Bible in years (*Absence from Felicity*, pg. 229).

In this instance, Jesus was telling Helen that reading the Bible was a way to examine his credentials, to become more familiar with the life he led, and with what gave him the authority to speak as he does in the Course. Admittedly, this was private guidance, and as such it does not automatically apply to everyone. Still, if Jesus urged Helen to read the Bible, it probably would be a good idea for many of us as well.

The Bible Contains Much Truth

As we've pointed out in this booklet, there is much in the Bible that is consonant with the Course. Obviously the Course does not quote everything it agrees with; there are many other statements of truth in the Bible that can help us, just as there is truth to be found in the Hindu scriptures, or Buddhist writings. Reading the Bible can be an inspiring supplement to the Course.

In addition, the Bible is your heritage; there is more reason for a Course student to read the Bible than to read other scriptures. For a Course student to read the Bible is, to me, much like a Christian reading the Old Testament: you know that it has been superseded, and yet you recognize your roots there. This is the history of your spiritual family, so to speak. If you are unfamiliar with the Bible, but know the Course, when you read the Bible you will probably be surprised at how many things seem familiar because you have seen them in the Course. Likewise, if you are familiar with the Bible and read the Course, you will find the Course taking your Bible knowledge and using it to carry you to levels of understanding you never dreamed of while reading only the Bible, and you will understand what the Course is saying more quickly than someone with no knowledge of the Bible.

The Bible is Called the Source of Truth

In *Absence From Felicity*, Jesus is quoted as having made the following remarks:

> Contradictions in My words mean lack of understanding, or scribal failures, which I make every effort to correct. But they are still not crucial. The Bible has the same problem, I assure you, and it's still being edited. Consider the power of My Word, in that it has withstood all the attacks of error, and is the Source of Truth (*Absence from Felicity*, pp. 231-232).

Jesus clearly associates his efforts to transmit truth through Helen and the Course to earlier efforts to transmit revelation which resulted in the Bible. He says the Bible "has the same problem" of "scribal errors," which are being corrected to this day. (I think he is referring to the continual efforts of biblical scholars to arrive at the purest possible early manuscripts and better translations of them.) The last sentence then refers to "My Word," with a clear implication that the Bible either *is* or *contains* that Word. Jesus draws our attention to how that Word, despite repeated attacks of error (corrupted manuscripts, scribal errors, and mistranslations), has yet remained "the Source of Truth." In other words, the truth is in there for those with eyes to see past the scribal errors and find it. If Jesus himself has such a high opinion of the Bible, and says that it contains his "Word," Course students should be able to find much benefit from reading it.

HOW SHOULD WE INTERPRET THE BIBLE?

My basic rule of thumb for Course students reading the Bible would be: Interpret the Bible as the Course interprets it. The following all seem significant to me:

Be Aware That It is Imperfect

The Course obviously regards the Bible as imperfect, as we have seen. Be aware of that as you read. As Jesus told us in the Course, "As you read the teachings of the Apostles, remember that I told them myself that there was much they would understand later, because they were not wholly ready to follow me at the time" (T-6.I.16:1). Therefore, you cannot take everything in the Bible as "the Gospel truth" (sorry for the pun). Some of what the Bible says came from the limited understanding of the Apostles. Be aware of how the Course differs from the Bible, and as you read, set aside those things that seem to clearly contradict what you know from the Course.

Be Ready to Reinterpret in Light of ACIM

Another way we've seen the Course treat the Bible is by reinterpreting it, or "spiritualizing" it. "Vengeance is mine" becomes a way of telling us to give up vengeance, rather than informing us that God carries it out. If something in the Bible strikes you as discordant with the truth of the Course, rather than simply ignoring it or throwing it out, you can try, with the Holy Spirit's help, reinterpreting it in a way that does fit the Course.

As an example, take the story of Jesus chasing the money-changers out of the Temple (see Matt. 21:12-13). Many people have interpreted this story in a way that has Jesus becoming angry, losing his temper, and behaving in a rather egoic way. It does say he overthrew tables, so he certainly wasn't being very meek and gentle. Many Christians have taught, using this story as a basis, that there is such a thing as "righteous anger." Yet the Course teaches, "Anger is never justified" (T-30.VI.1:1). So you may want to find an interpretation of this story that somehow agrees with the Course. You may decide Jesus did what he did as a teaching example, without getting angry. You may decide this story isn't to be trusted at all, and that Jesus never did those things. What you *do not* do is allow the Bible to take higher authority, and to override the teaching of the Course, which is that anger is *never* justified.

Reject Anything Clearly Based on Fear

One clear indicator of things in the Bible to beware of are any of its teachings that are quite clearly based on fear—such as threats of God's vengeance, God's wrath, or hell—things the Course vehemently rejects as stemming purely from our own fear and our projection onto God. Jesus says that the real message of the Gospel is only the message of love, and fear is love's opposite.

The ego, the Course tells us, is simply a fearful thought (T-5.V.3:7). If we listen to our own egos as we read the Bible, we will see it through a filter of fear, and even the *good* parts will become fearful in some way:

> Nothing the ego perceives is interpreted correctly. Not only does the ego cite Scripture for its purpose, but it even interprets Scripture as a witness for itself. The Bible is a fearful thing in the ego's judgment. Perceiving it as frightening, it interprets it fearfully (T-5.VI.4:3-6).

Remember that fearful thoughts and the ego are identical. If what you are reading arouses fear, your ego is doing the interpreting. Stop, be still, and ask the Holy Spirit to interpret for you. If you are too agitated (and there are some fearful things in the Bible!), perhaps putting the Bible aside for a while would be best. In fact, if reading *the Course* becomes associated with fear (and I have known a few people for whom this has happened), it might be good to stop reading the Course as well. Remember that healing is escape from fear (T-2.IV.1:7); if something increases your fear, it isn't helping!

Ask the Help of the Holy Spirit

If we ask Him, the Holy Spirit will help us reinterpret the Bible in a way that coincides with the Course. Remember that He is with us to assist us as we read, and to show us His loving interpretations, just as He did with many of the examples we have examined in this booklet.

Remember, too, the ways in which He reinterprets things, and look for that kind of answer. He consistently interprets so as to picture a God Who is purely loving and not punitive. He changes thoughts that seem to show judgment upon *sinful people* into thoughts that speak of eliminating *mistaken thoughts* of our minds. He emphasizes changing our minds rather than changing our behavior. He consistently denies any reality to separation, and reinforces the fact of our eternal and unbreakable union with God. As we read and ask His help, we will find Him following these same patterns in the reinterpretations He gives to us.

When we read the Bible, then, we should always ask His help to see it as He sees it, and to understand it as He understands it.

Do Not Expect Any Perfect Reconciliation

My final word of advice to Course students about the Bible is: Don't expect to be able to perfectly reconcile them. I hope, after reading the chapter on *Differences*, this will be obvious to everyone who reads this. The teaching of the Bible and the teaching of the Course are not the same, and there is no way you can reinterpret everything in the Bible to make it fit the Course, or vice versa.

The Bible, from Genesis to Revelation, is based on the concept that separation from God is real. Nearly everything it teaches is colored by that error. The Course declares that the separation never happened, and everything it teaches is based on that truth. The resulting thought systems, taken as whole thought systems, cannot be reconciled because they differ at their roots.

There are many *pieces* of the Bible thought system, however, that do fit within the context of the Course's thought system. In fact, despite its wholly erroneous presupposition of the reality of separation, sin, and God's wrath, the Bible does a remarkably good job of presenting a message of love and forgiveness. Finding those points of agreement should be our goal in reading the Bible. It is these points of agreement, by the way, that will help foster friendly relations between Course students and devoted Bible students, and that will enable some Course students who desire to do so to function happily within the context of a church or synagogue. I have often found, for instance, that relating to Christians on the basis of a shared relationship with Jesus brought about a feeling of unity between us, despite theological differences.

SEEING THE BIBLE DIFFERENTLY

To wrap things up as simply as I can, let me suggest that how a Course student should see the Bible is almost exactly how the Course asks us to see everything: through the eyes of Christ, using the judgment of the Holy Spirit.

All around us is a world that seems to engender fear in us. Everything seems to be some kind of threat or attack. The latest thing I have heard somewhere is that peanut butter can kill you! Most especially there are *people* who appear to be attacking us: competing with us, trying to take our belongings (or our spouses), doing us bodily injury, cheating us, plotting against us, lying to us, betraying us. The Course advocates one solution for all: forgiveness. It tells us we need to learn to look on everything and everyone in the world through the eyes of forgiveness. The judgment of the Holy Spirit can be given to us, if we ask, enabling us to see that:

> Every loving thought is true. Everything else is an appeal for
> healing and help, regardless of the form it takes (T-12.I.3:3-4).

The Course contends that what we all are is love, and that the ego does not exist. Our assignment in this world is to learn to see past the illusion of egoity to the Son of God that lies hidden underneath, in everyone. What looks like attack *can* be seen as an appeal for help, or a call for love, as it is referred to elsewhere in the same section. Sometimes what looks like attack can actually be a distorted expression of love; anger can be motivated by a desire for joining; someone trying to make me guilty can be seen as the ego's mistaken attempt to win my love. The Holy Spirit can always find love in whatever He looks upon, and He helps us to do the same; He sees only the love as true, and everything else is but an appeal for love.

The Holy Spirit has the job of translating our perceptions from fearful ones to perceptions of love. He does the translating; we do not. Our part is to be willing to see things differently, and to ask for His help; He then gives the transformed perception to us. He is called "the great Transformer of perception" (T-17.II.5:2), "the reinterpreter of what the ego made" (T-5.III.11:1). The Course tells us, "The Holy Spirit will help you reinterpret everything that you perceive as fearful, and teach you that only what is loving is true" (T-5.IV.1:3).

What does all this have to do with how we see the Bible? We are to look upon the Bible in exactly the same way as we are asked to look on everything. I believe that we can boil everything I've said in this booklet down to simply this:

To see the Bible differently means to learn to forgive the Bible: To be willing to lay aside our perceptions based on fear, and to ask the Holy Spirit to help us interpret the Bible as He sees it, learning to set aside what stems from fear, retaining only the love; so that where once in the Bible we saw God's wrath, our own guilt, and much cause for fear, we now see only God's love.

The following remarks from the Course about how we try to use words to communicate, and so often fail because the ego's addiction to separateness so often twists our words, seems particularly applicable to the ways the Holy Spirit can help us find God's truth in the Bible:

> Yet even this strange and twisted effort to communicate through not communicating holds enough of love to make it meaningful if its Interpreter is not its maker. You who made it are but expressing conflict, from which the Holy Spirit would release you....He will interpret it to you with perfect clarity, for He knows with Whom you are in perfect communication.

> You know not what you say, and so you know not what is said to you. Yet your Interpreter perceives the meaning in your alien language. He will not attempt to communicate the meaningless. But He will separate out all that has meaning, dropping off the rest... (T-14.VI.6:4-7:4).

Even though the egos of the biblical authors have distorted God's revelation, even though in some cases they are actually expressing conflict instead of peace, the Holy Spirit can interpret it for us "with perfect clarity," separating out the part He refers to as "enough of love," which is the only part that gives it meaning, and dropping off the rest. The Holy Spirit can help us reinterpret the Bible, and everything we perceive as fearful in the Bible, and can teach us that only what is loving is true, just as He is doing with the rest of our lives.

Booklets in this Series Based on *A COURSE IN MIRACLES*
by Robert Perry and Allen Watson

1. **Seeing the Face of Christ in All Our Brothers** *by Robert*. How we can see the Presence of God in others.

2. **Special Relationships: Illusions of Love** *by Robert*. Explains the unconscious motives that drive our seemingly loving relationships, and describes methods for transforming them into something holy.

3. **Shrouded Vaults of the Mind** *by Robert*. Draws a map of the mind based on ACIM, and takes you on a tour through its many levels.

4. **Guidance: Living the Inspired Life** *by Robert*. Sketches an overall perspective on guidance and its place on the spiritual path.

5. **Holy Relationships: The End of an Ancient Journey** *by Robert*. Traces the stages of the holy relationship, as it develops from its modest beginnings to its sublime completion.

6. **Reality & Illusion: An Overview of Course Metaphysics, Part I** *by Robert*. Examines the Course's vision of reality. With Booklet #7, forms a comprehensive overview of ACIM's metaphysical thought system.

7. **Reality & Illusion: An Overview of Course Metaphysics, Part II** *by Robert*. Discusses the origins of our apparent separation from God.

8. **A Healed Mind Does Not Plan** *by Allen*. Examines our approach to planning and decision-making, showing how it is possible to leave the direction of our lives up to the Holy Spirit.

9. **Through Fear To Love** *by Allen*. Explores two sections from A Course in Miracles that deal with our fear of redemption. Leads the reader to see how it is possible to look upon ourselves with love.

10. **The Journey Home** *by Allen*. Presents a description of our spiritual destination and what we must go through to get there.

11. **Everything You Always Wanted to Know About Judgment but Were Too Busy Doing It to Notice** *by Robert and Allen*. A survey of various teaching about judgment in ACIM.

12. **The Certainty of Salvation** *by Robert and Allen*. How we can become certain that we will find our way to God.

13. **What is Death?** *by Allen*. The Course's view of what death really is.

14. **The Workbook as a Spiritual Practice** *by Robert*. A guide for getting the most out of the Workbook.

15. **I Need Do Nothing: Finding the Quiet Center** *by Allen*. An in-depth discussion of one of the most misunderstood parts of the Course.

16. **A Course Glossary** *by Robert*. 158 definitions of terms and phrases from *A Course in Miracles* for beginning students, more experienced students, and study groups.